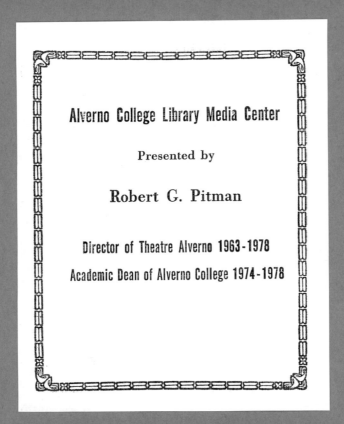

TO A YOUNG ACTRESS

TO A YOUNG ACTRESS

THE LETTERS OF
BERNARD SHAW
TO
MOLLY TOMPKINS

*The correspondence between
Bernard Shaw and an American artist from 1921 through 1949*

ILLUSTRATED WITH PHOTOGRAPHS

EDITED AND WITH AN INTRODUCTION BY

PETER TOMPKINS

Clarkson N. Potter, Inc./Publisher

NEW YORK

Library of Congress Catalogue Card Number: 60-11493

DESIGNED BY CHRISTOPHER SIMON

MANUFACTURED IN THE UNITED STATES OF AMERICA
BY
BOOK CRAFTSMEN ASSOCIATES, INC.,
NEW YORK

First Edition

INTRODUCTION

The letters reproduced in this volume were written by Bernard Shaw to Molly Tompkins from 1921—when she was twenty-four and he sixty-five—to 1949, a span of twenty-eight years.

Molly Tompkins, the great-granddaughter of Timothy Shea Arthur, publisher of *Arthur's Magazine* and author of that curious tale of Americana, *Ten Nights in a Bar Room,* was born in New York City and brought up in Georgia as Mary Arthur. When she arrived in London in the summer of 1921 with her sculptor husband and two-year-old son, her acting career consisted of a twelve-week engagement at an old Broadway theater where she had walked across the stage, for the benefit of Mr. Ziegfeld and his *Follies,* not unlike one of the racing fans in the Ascot scene of *My Fair Lady.*

Her husband, Laurence Tompkins, then in his twenty-third year, having courted her at a Beaux Arts Ball in New York and taken her home to Georgia to be married, was preoccupied with designing a Shavian Theater on whose Romanesque façade he planned to carve in stone the story of Shaw's creative evolution.

The young couple's purpose in going to England was to find Bernard Shaw.

There, they decided, was a prophet with a social philosophy and a religion of creative evolution who alone could redeem the world and humanize and enlighten its people sufficiently to live together in peace and happiness, yet he was crying in the wilderness, decried as a mountebank and dangerous revolutionary.

To remedy this negligence, they counted on their Shavian Theater, from which the prophet's gospel could be disseminated cheaply to the world: Laurence Tompkins would see to its construction, Molly Tompkins would interpret the prophet's message by becoming a Shavian actress.

Not knowing where to find Shaw, whose name was not listed in the telephone directory, they wheedled it from a clerk at Hatchard's, one of London's old bookshops.

When they found Shaw at Adelphi Terrace, his advice to her, if she wished to become a professional actress, was immediately to enroll in the Royal Academy of Dramatic Art, on Gower Street; to him: get a studio and set to work.

Both followed Shaw's advice. He gave more. The more he gave the more they seemed to need. He invited them to lunch at Adelphi Terrace to meet amusing people, showed them where to go for walks in the countryside of England, took them separately to enjoy different sights of London: Laurence to exhibitions of painting and sculpture, to his clubs, to the Royal Automobile Club pool for a daily swim; Molly to the theater and the cinema, to tea at the houses of his colleagues Galsworthy and Barrie.

Soon he was taking them on tours of England, bounding along its lanes in his high open car driving at sixty miles an hour from one cathedral town to the next, pointing out the sights and the beauties, singing snatches of opera at the top of his voice.

Using them as buffers to protect himself from overzealous disciples at the Fabian Summer Schools he still made it a duty to visit, he dragged them happily from one end of England to the other, from Surrey to Yorkshire, from Essex to Somerset.

In Italy he went to see them at their island on Lake Maggiore, where day by day he could swim, play, listen to music, go on picnics, discover antiquities, climb the nearby hills, enjoy the fun and beauty of life, in the evenings substitute for his "regular" menus the wholesome food of a *trattoria,* sit undisturbed in the little village cinemas among the rain-damp sweaty peasant audience and laugh at Charlie Chaplin—in his own words "have a jolly good time."

With them he could say what he pleased on any subject of interest—and there seemed to be none that wasn't—without having to choose his words for effect; what's more, he could, and would, be told he was wrong, ill-informed, old-fashioned, out-of-date, be treated, that is, like a human being instead of that figure of his own creation: The Great G.B.S.!

Thus developed a correspondence in which Shaw began by counseling Molly Tompkins on how to speak and to act, how to dress and make up, how to handle theatrical managers, write a fine hand, paint pictures, write plays, and, above all, master the art of saying a plain "No!" Counsel followed counsel till in the end he was telling her how to keep or lose a husband, how to bring up a child, get on with a daughter-in-law, care for the schooling of grandchildren.

Not all of Shaw's letters are available: some are lost, some were destroyed, one whole batch was taken by a person who hoped to use them for profit.

Of Shaw's fifty or sixty letters to Laurence only one is extant. The others, entrusted to a traveler returning to the States, were never seen again.

Of Molly's letters to Shaw—and she must have written him close to a thousand—not a trace. They do not appear to be among either the catalogued or uncatalogued boxes in care of the British Museum. Miss Blanche Patch, Shaw's secretary throughout the correspondence, who saw most of the letters arrive, believes that Shaw destroyed them before he died.

There was no sign of them at Shaw's flat in Whitehall or at his country house in Hertfordshire, though the guardian in whose care it was left combed the house from rafters to cellar.

The presumption must be that they are lost.

They would have clarified references to persons, places, and incidents mentioned in Shaw's letters, they might have been delightful to read in context—Shaw maintained that her natural talent was writing—yet they would not serve to alter a comma of what Shaw wrote.

To make up for this lack, Shaw's letters could have been annotated, page by page, with an essay on every one; but so much would have to be said for the benefit of those who know nothing of Shaw that would be redundant to Shavian enthusiasts that the letters are best left stand on their own.

The purpose of this volume is not to tell the story of a little known side of Shaw's life—his happy relations with an American family: this may appear elsewhere—but to make available to the scholar and the interested public a collection of Shavian writings that show the dramatist-philosopher in another light.

For years I watched the steady flow of small square envelopes, off-gray or pale blue, written in the playwright's spidery hand or tapped out by the keys of his poorly ribboned typewriter, addressed to Paris or Sicily, the Balearics or Dalmatia, along with postcards exotically stamped from all over the world, as they accumulated in the bottom of a seventeenth-century Venetian chest, battered by much travel and often nearly lost; the war years it spent in the Renaissance cellar of a Roman palazzo in the company of some hand grenades and a secret OSS radio, and that it was saved for shipment to the United States is due entirely to the devotion of the Italians to whom it was entrusted.

At any time since the war the letters could have been destroyed by fire, theft, or unforeseen event—and been lost forever.

As there is nothing in the letters that could harm any person living or dead, I finally bucked the family tendency to reserve and had the letters photostated. Because of the not unreasonable legal device that grants to the author of a letter its copyright and to the recipient its physical property, the permission of the Shaw Estate was necessary and this I obtained through the Society of Authors.

Those who saw the photostats were so pleased with the added visual quality of reading the letters in Shaw's own hand, with insertions and postscripts, it seemed worth while taking the trouble to reproduce as many of them as possible by the present process of photolithography. That Shaw would have approved this system, preoccupied as he was all his life, and especially in his last years, with avoiding the colossal waste of labor involved in transcribing and setting into type communications in our superannuated alphabet and barbaric method of spelling, I am reasonably sure.

In any case, it is thanks to the foresight and confidence of the publisher, Mr. Clarkson Potter, that these letters are now available in the present special edition, and I trust they will charm and amuse the reader as much as they are dear to my mother, Molly Tompkins, to whom they were addressed.

Peter Tompkins

Washington, D. C.
April 1960

TO A YOUNG ACTRESS

AYOT ST LAWRENCE,WELWYN,HERTS.
STATION.WHEATHAMPSTEAD, G.N.R.2¼ MILES.
TELEGRAMS:BERNARD SHAW,CODICOTE.

10 ADELPHI TERRACE.W.C 2.

27th December 1921.

My dear Mollytompkins

What a shocking little fraud you are, pretending to have read all my books; when you havnt read one of them. When I was a young thing, I, too, was quite distressed because my work was not perfect. I compared my beginnings with other people's endings, and couldnt help noticing a painful difference. I was clearly not living up to the precept "Be ye perfect, even as your father in heaven is perfect". Nowadays I perceive that even HE is not perfect.

Well, I made myself a workman by slaving away for five years writing clumsy novels ; and in the last of them I described the discouragement my heroine suffered because she was not perfect and because the hero wouldnt be heroic. Now I did that to help people over the Slough of Despond in which I had wallowed ; and if you had read it you would not be such a very silly Mollytompkins as you are, with your nonsense about perfection and about my wanting perfect actresses. I dont cry for the moon, and am only too glad when I can strike the least little spark out of the stars I have to put up with.

Now I will tell you something about your little performance. I do not think you have much to learn that can be taught in school by an ordinary teacher. You will have to acquire the English alphabet in Gower St : you still have very queer Rs from the cockney standpoint, and one or two other letters that will bear polishing. Dont pick up smart English, which is bad English : all you need do is to drop certain provincialisms. However your Welsh instructor will take care of that : University College is not Oxford, thank heaven ! For the rest, what you want is work, or rather sheer drudgery to put up your muscle, and give you the hard driven professional touch that comes from doing a thing every day for ten years and in no other way. Without that, although you may know how a thing should be done, and understand it a thousand times better than a hack fifty-dollar-a-week actress, she will "get it across" more effectively than you. I dont know whether you are a musician. If not, you dont know Mozart : and if you dont know Mozart you will never understand my technique. If you are, you must have noticed sometime or another that though a composer may play his music ever so much more beautifully and intelligently than a profes-

The "little performance" was a modern comedy, *Clothes and the Woman,* directed by Claude Rains, in which M.T. played the part of a slavey in the first act, who turns into the heroine in the second; as it was the first play performed by her class on the R.A.D.A. (Royal Academy of Dramatic Art) stage, each student was allowed to invite two guests: hers were Shaw and Laurence T.

sional pianist, yet he cannot produce the same effect in a concert room, because he hasnt got the steel in his fingers. You have to get steel in the muscles of your face, and steel in your heart, by hammering away every day (or night) until you can hit the boy at the back of the gallery in a three hundred pound house. Dont think that at present you can reach only three rows of stalls, and that as you go on you will carry a row further and yet another row until you get to the wall. That's not it at all. You can reach the boy all right now, just as you can reach the conductor of the band. But you xxnf can't take possession of him and hold him up above the discomfort of his cheap seat.

If you go through with the school, I have no doubt you will get the gold medal easily enough if you have any luck. I discovered that you are really pretty. I could not be certain of that before ; because you are as vain as a goldfinch, and make up your face and lips, and throw yourself at the people in the street as a beauty in a scandalous manner. Make-up cuts no ice with me : what would you think of me if you met me in the Strand with my lips painted ? But grace and a fine shape cannot be simulated in the dresses you wore in the play ; and I found that you have both.

I hadnt time to write to you at once, and really havnt time now ;but you have softened my stony heart a little ; and now I suppose I am in for taking some interest in you occasionally. Only, if you love me, dont ask me to answer letters oftener than once in a blue moon. You see, writing is my professional job ; and when my day's work is done I am written out, and would rather die than form another sentence.

Give my regards to poor Tompkins : he has taken on a fine handfull.

ever,

G. Bernard Shaw

P.S. My secretary hasnt sent me down your letter with your address in it ; so I must send this to Gower St. Please send me a card with the address to me here in the country.

PPS My dog has chewed up my fountain pen ; and I can't write with this thing.

The Postscript reads:

P.S. My secretary hasn't sent me down your letter with your address in it; so I must send this to Gower St. Please send me a card with the address to me here in the country.

P.P.S. My dog has chewed up my fountain pen; and I can't write with this thing.

AYOT ST LAWRENCE, WELWYN, HERTS.
STATION: WHEATHAMPSTEAD, G.N.R. 2¼ MILES.
TELEGRAMS: BERNARD SHAW, CODICOTE.

9th Jan 1922

10 ADELPHI TERRACE. W.C.2.

Gracious God, child, what is this?

A letter from a young actress to a great playwright, addressed Mister !!!! Whole careers have been wrecked by blunders of that sort. Do it again to any manager, any author, any person whatsoever who conceives himself to be a gentleman, and you are lost for ever. It is the blackest, deadliest, unpardonablest of insults in England.

What is more, it is so unusual that the man's wife gets the letter and opens it, because the Mr is assumed to be a carelessly written

14

Mrs .

Know, Mollytompkins, that I am .

Bernard Shaw Esquire (or Esq. or ⟨symbol⟩ , or ⟨symbol⟩)

but never Mister Bernard Shaw. Your tradesmen are Misters; but all the people you have to flatter or be polite to are Esquires.

Your husband is Horatio Tompkins Esquire; and you are (on an envelope) Mrs Horatio Tompkins .

Be VERY particular about this; and remember that Pinero is Sir Arthur Pinero pure and simple; but Barrie is Sir James Barrie, Bart. O.M. I know a man who was ruined because he spelt Lord Rosebary's name Roseberry .

Some day I shall take your face and scrub it and show you that it looks much better unbuttered .

AYOT ST LAWRENCE,WELWYN,HERTS.
STATION:WHEATHAMPSTEAD,G.N.R.2¼ MILES
TELEGRAMS:BERNARD SHAW,CODICOTE.

10 ADELPHI TERRACE.W.C.2.

11th January 1922.

Dear Mollytomkins

When you get a bit of advice, dont bolt it. Chew it fortyseven times ; and then it will digest all right.

When you call on a manager with a eye to an engagement, lay it on as thick as you please, because one of the things he wants to know is whether you can make up stage-pretty. But in private life dont give away your professional secrets. Leave the shop at home, and make everyone say "Is that ugly devil the lovely Mollytomkins ? My ! she must be clever."

Remember that in England you are not homely : you are plain. Homely here means domesticated. Also, you get buried in a coffin, and not in a casket ; and you qualify yourself for the operation by becoming a body or a corpse, not a cadaver. And the word nude is not considered more polite than naked. And you cannot stand this or that, not "stand for" this or that. And Duse is an Italian, not a Dago.

But what do you mean by proposing to interview managers and seek engagements before you have got rid of your Amurricanisms in Gower St? Dont you know that they will just say "Half baked little American girl : pretty ; but no good : awful accent and no drive in her! And it may take you years to get over that false start. You just wait for another six months to get your mouth straight and your muscle up. Then beat the villages with The Arts League of Service for a while : they play the first act of Arms & The Man as a whole play ; and Eleanor Elder, who runs it, is a friend of mine. And keep your figure and dont live on chocolate creams more than you can help.

Dont learn music : listen to it. And dont expect to like it until you can whistle the tunes, and dance them. You do dance, dont you ?

Now you have got another letter out of me by saying that silly thing about not making up for the managers. And yet you have the face to pretend that you love me.

In great haste

The Arts League of Service was a group of traveling artists who toured the remoter parts of England giving varied programs of mimed folk music, dances, short plays and sketches, to stimulate local interest in the drama. Under the direction of Eleanor Elder, an actress in Granville-Barker's company who had switched to dancing, they had great freedom in choice of material and in experimentation.

27th January 1922

THE ALBANY,

HASTINGS.

Dear Mollytompkins

That is quite as it should be — I think you would be charming as the water; but you could shew off your phonetics as Phil, who is generally represented as a lout, but ought to be the last word in precocious elegance & finish.

Who is the teacher?

I am glad the phonetics are useful; but as the College laboratory is the only institution of the kind I know, I don't see how you are to change.

Afterall and Westminsterabbey may have to be unlearned for the stage, as the coup de glotte before a vowel, German fashion, is often necessary for emphasis, audibility in a big house, and giving value to a metric foot in verse. However, do not bother about anything being right or wrong: what you need is to become conscious of what you are doing. When you know the differences, you can use your own taste and judgment. Wot, wich, were, wen, weel &c. are absolutely incorrect; but the alternatives hwat, hwich, hwere, hwen, and hweel are equally incorrect, though they are the speech of Ada Rehan and Forbes Robertson, the best speakers

The R.A.D.A. required its students to play many different roles in different plays. The teachers were actors on the London stage who used their mornings to rehearse the students. Shaw, on the board of directors, helped finance and took a great interest in the R.A.D.A. for almost half a century.

you could find on the stage. A genuine wh is hard to
execute and hard to catch: babies dont pick it up from their
mothers because they cant hear it and that she is saying wot,
wen &c; but they do hear and pick up the hw, which
prevails in the north, in Scotland, in Ireland & in America,
and is in fact standard English speech. I use it.

When I first heard Don Giovanni practised (I didnt see it
regularly performed) I thought the music trivial, rapid, and
colorless, being accustomed at the time to Italian music of the
Verdi sort. I have never heard a really good complete performance:
there never will be one until everybody, from the drummer upwards,
knows his part by heart and never has to look at a book or at
the conductor. Strauss wants me to go to Salzburg to hear him conduct it.

But the reason the violoncellos didnt palpitate in a ghostly
way was that you were listening to the real music and not to
the ghost of it.

Anyhow, you dont get masterpieces quite so cheap as you
expect when you are young. Mozart can afford to wait. You are
right about the story. It is disgusting: Beethoven said he couldnt
understand how M. could set it. He didnt, in fact: the music
tells quite another story. And the wretched incomplete band at the
Old Vic. couldnt play the music.

I dont know what possessed ~~Chesterton~~ Chesterton to say that I answered

To improve M.T.'s diction, Shaw sent her to Professor Daniel
Jones, who taught phonetics at London University, partly a pro-
totype of Higgins in *Pygmalion*.

Ada Rehan was a very popular Irish-born American actress
who died in 1916.

letters. What he meant was that ③ he doesn't.

That was a magnificent swank going to school without the make-up. Nothing else that you could do will make an impression of superiority like that. I am impressed. I shall begin to believe in you presently.

But how could he be so silly as to go and pay ten & sixpence for that photograph when you might have come to Adelphi Terrace and rummaged the press into which all the copies the photographers send me are stuck. Your countryman Alvin Langdon Coburn has lots that he has taken of me. If you had written him a letter six pages long about me and told him he was the greatest photographer in the world and that you were a very very poor girl who adores me (slow music) it would have cost you only a twopenny stamp and a haporth of paper, and he would perhaps have sent you a really nice one. Next time you want anything I am likely to have kicking about the place, ask me for it.

Dont say yours for ever in my plays or I will never love you any more. But they cant mean that really. They might as well teach you to say Maraman, which is quite English. I have heard a Morell say "either Candida is mad, or else —

You see you have extorted another letter. But then I am having a day or two at the seaside to amuse myself; and you are a very insinuating Mollytompkins.

Sir Johnston Forbes-Robertson was England's idol of the stage, from which he retired in 1913.

The Strauss referred to is Richard, a close friend of Shaw's. The Chesterton is G.K.

The Albany was chosen for me, not by me; but they feed me well. All that is necessary in a hotel is to ask for one special dish for lunch or dinner — maccaroni or spaghetti, butter beans, sweet corn, curried eggs, Yorkshire pudding or what not — and the rest of the meal like anyone else. You must be very careful how you change. Merely omitting meat, fish, & fowl, without replacing them by equally nutritious substitutes will result in early death. Above all, dont suppose that vegetarianism means eating vegetables: I dont eat more vegetables than carnivorous people do. Cabbage and rice pudding wont do. Dont be scientific and stuff yourself with loathly lentils because they are nitrogenous; but make yourself comfortable somehow.

Was it at the New Inn I lunched that frightfully cold Tuesday? I like Wincholsea.

For Y.N.C.T. dont muddle about mid-Victorian costumes: take the exact date (1895?) and look up the volumes of Punch for that year: the Du Maurier pictures will give you the fashions. Perhaps I could talk to you about it some afternoon, next week: I shall be in town from Wednesday to Saturday. What are your free hours? G.B.S.

Printed in left margin:
10 ADELPHI TERRACE. W.C.2.
AYOT ST LAWRENCE, WELWYN, HERTS. 15th Oct 1922
STATION: WHEATHAMPSTEAD, G.N.R. 2¼ MILES.
TELEGRAMS: BERNARD SHAW, CODICOTE.

Y.N.C.T. is Shaw's *You Never Can Tell*, first produced in London in 1899. M.T. was to play the part of Gloria in an R.A.D.A. performance for which Shaw gave her special coaching at Adelphi Terrace.

L.T. was trying to convince M.T. to become a vegetarian. Shaw, who believed in exercise, gave them a booklet on walks within fifty miles of London and each week end, rain or shine, they set off on a new one.

20

Dolly, Mrs. Clandon, and Gloria are all
characters in Shaw's *You Never Can Tell*.
K.B. is Kenneth Barnes, principal of the
R.A.D.A. with whom Shaw watched M.T.'s
performance.

The Malvern Hotel. Great Malvern, Worcs. 20th Ap. 1922

No, Mollytompkins : certainly not. Never write letters : they only make mischief. (And how often must I tell you to date them when you *do* write them?) Of course you are not to be depended on, and dont know what to do or what not to do : that is the disadvantage of youth ; but as some sage has remarked " Youth, which forgives itself nothing, is forgiven everything ; whilst age, which forgives itself everything, is forgiven nothing". Education in the ways of the world is a series of humiliations, like learning to skate. All you can do is to laugh at yourself with the crowd.

Perhaps there would be no harm in writing " Dear Mr Barnes : It seems that I have done something dreadful as to you and Mr Bernard Shaw. Of course he never told me to tell you anything ; but I thought in my innocence that it would be more persuasive if I put it that way. Please make allowances : I shall be more careful next time ; and I am very sorry — contritely — Mary Arthur ". Mind : I dont advise you to write at all ; but if you feel you must, that is the best you can do. Anyhow, he may talk to you about it ; and that is all you can say. You seem to be able to handle him very successfully without any prompting ; so I need say no more about it.

You will grow out of your Shavian infatuation (alas ! for I hope it is a great pleasure to you) ; but

Kenneth Barnes, later Sir K., principal of the R.A.D.A. from 1909 till 1955, was the brother of the two English actresses Irene and Violet Vanburgh. M.T. fought with him continually because he insisted that she play all sorts of parts, especially comedy, whereas she wanted to do nothing but tragic parts; in their association she must have been as big a trial to him with her non-conformism as he was to her with his academic trappings.

meanwhile don't blither. The Duke of Wellington would have said "Don't be a damned fool"; but I have not the heart.

V. B. says they can teach you a lot more, and that you are irregular in your attendance. It is up to the Academy to interest you enough to make you regular; but give it a chance.

LES MAITRES DE L'ESTAMPE AU XVIIIᵉ SIÈCLE

L'ÉCUREUSE

L'ŒUVRE DE CHARDIN
Gravure de C.-N. Cochin

ND Phot

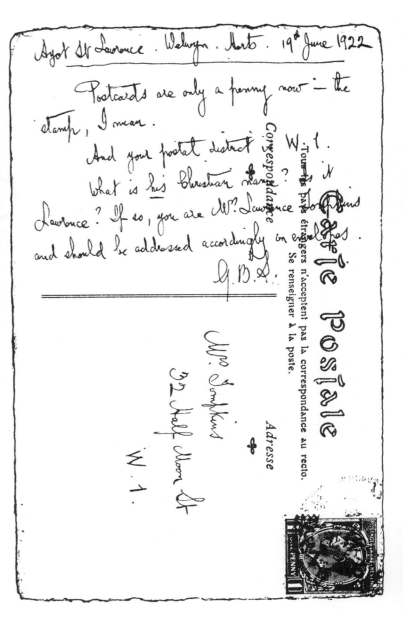

Ayot St Lawrence. Welwyn. Herts. 19ᵗʰ June 1922

Postcards are only a penny now — the stamp, I mean.

And your postal district W.1.

What is his Christian name?

Lawrence? If so, you are Mrs. Lawrence and should be addressed accordingly.

G. B. S.

Correspondance

Carte Postale

Tout les pays étrangers n'acceptent pas la correspondance au recto. Se renseigner à la poste.

Adresse

Mrs. Tompkins
32 Half Moon St
W. 1.

The Walton Park Hotel. Clevedon. Somerset. 16th July 1922

Mollytompkins, Mollytompkins

You are a disgrace to me. They lay all your sins on my shoulders; and when you behave like Sarah of Red Gulch instead of like the distinguished Mrs Lawrence Tompkins with a patent University College English accent, they come to me and ask me despairingly what they are to do with you and why I didnt bring you up properly. Then you get out of it with some beau geste or other; and I am asked to say nothing this time. You are worse than the tragedienne who rehearsed Pygmalion in the upper division for me some years ago, and then went and threw a glass of lemonade in the face of the female who catered for the students, and spoilt her niece's hat (the caterer ducked, and the niece got the lemonade). That cost her fourteen shillings, the value of the hat. Do you like the victims of your wrath?

Cant you muster up enough dignity to feel that you must not on any provocation whatever say things that are meant to be offensive and humiliating? If you had a sense of humor, I should suggest that when you are annoyed you should with unruffled cordiality knock the offender down or tell her cheerfully to go to hell; but you are not comedian enough to carry that off gracefully; so you must adopt the crueller but more dignified alternative of being imperturbably polite.

The director, to appease my demand on your behalf for tragic Shakespearean parts, spoke of Cleopatra; but Cleopatra is essentially a comedy part, and even a low comedy part in bits. Helena in All's Well, Isabella in Measure for Measure, Constance in King John (though she, too, is realistic; but you have that sort of bad temper: you dont abstain from bitter tongued resentment), Margaret in the Henry the Sixths, Cassandra in Troilus (half a dozen lines only), are the parts for you. Racine would have suited you very well if he had been English. Ask Mademoiselle to teach you Phèdre.

All my parts are comedy parts except Jennifer and Mrs Knox, as far as I can remember without going over my past like a drowning man.

You must not keep on confusing the appreciation and understanding of parts and plays with the ability to act them. If the two were the same faculty then Shakespear would have been a greater actor than Burbage, and I should be able to play Cleopatra better than you. An actor stands in much the same relation to an author as a carpenter or mason to an architect: he need not understand the entire design in the least; and he would not do his own part of the job any better for such understanding. Even if he were a greater architect than the architect for whom he was working he could

With Claude Rains, M.T. could not get along. To the principal he said he would rather resign than have her in his class. When Kenneth Barnes called her on the mat and told her that he would expel her if it weren't that she showed promise, she added fuel to the feud by answering: "Mr. Shaw would like you better if you did."

not do his work without learning it like the stupidest carpenter alive. Your comprehension of plays is a positive and serious hindrance to you: instead of eagerly sawing all sorts of wood for the sake of learning to saw, you refuse to saw anything except Spanish mahogany and rosewood; and the result will be that you will not get on as fast as the student who is interested, not in the wood, but in the sawing. Where do you suppose I should be now if I had refused to write about anybody less than Dante or Goethe or Molière or Shakespear or Michael Angelo or Mozart? You must take on all sorts of jobs until you are perfectly handy at doing anything you want to with your instrument, which is your face plus your figure plus your voice.

I must not begin a fresh sheet: I have to start for Glastonbury in ten minutes. I shall be at this address until the 21st.

G.B.S.

The reverse of the postcard reads:

You are muddling up Measure for Measure with Cymbeline. There is nothing for your soul in Shakespear (though to do him justice he did not write Titus); but there is plenty of pasting for your ear; and you need an exquisite ear for tragedy. Mrs. Siddons thrilled a shop assistant by asking "Will it wash?": you must learn to do the same, even at the cost of studying old English plays that are morally disgusting. Have you read Ibsen's plays? You must: ignorance of them is out of the question for a modern actress with a cultural equipment.

I told you long ago to find out the Arts League of Service and do some work with them if Judith Wogan and Eleanor Elder will let anyone else in.

GBS

Llwyn. Harbsh. N. Wales (until the 16th)
12th Sept. 1922

Dear Mollytompkins

Thank you for the box of chocolates. It was so much too beautiful for me that I carefully wrapped it up again and presented it gallantly to my wife's hostess here, an American lady, who was much touched by your kindness, which she supposed to be mine.

I missed you greatly at Chester, where I slept on the way hither. You and Lawrence would have wallowed in the city walls, the old timbered houses, and all the rest of it.

You must not abandon Barnes until you have completed your course and taken your diploma (possibly your gold medal). Georgia will not believe a word of your tall stories about London unless you have this credential, which will bear my signature among the others. Besides, the work there, much as you despise it, has done you a lot of good; and you are not yet finished. If you could get a tour with the Arts League of Service, it would only be an interruption: you could return to Gower St. & complete your course there afterwards. But it would be better to go through with it straight on. To back out now would be defeat, failure, inconstancy, and spoilt good-for-nothingness. You really need more academic work. When I read your announcement that you were giving in, I used frightful language.

I start for home (Ayot St. Lawrence, Welwyn, Herts.) on Saturday morning, but shall not arrive until Monday evening.

ever,

G. Bernard Shaw.

Ayot St. Lawrence, Welwyn, Herts.
27th Sept. 1922.

Dear Mollytompkins

A bank official, above the rank of porter, had better be esquired.

One reason why your letters are not impressive is that your handwriting has no character: it might be anybody's. You should get a book on lettering and handwriting, and acquire a beautiful Italian script just as you are—or should be—acquiring a beautiful way of speaking. Who would answer that sloppy scrawl from a stranger? I have a book on the subject somewhere. If I can find it I will send it to you. You should see Ellen Terry's handwriting, or May Morris's. Mrs. Lang, by the way, can write your head off—: She has a prize handwriting.

Has Bassett Lowke sent you his snapshots of us?

It is no use asking me whether you are any good to me. How can I tell as long as you are an unfinished article? You dont exist as yet. Neither I nor any other mortal can tell whether you will be more than another Mary Anderson. Mary had quite a career: she had good looks and grace and had learned what could be learnt ambitiously and industriously; but she wouldnt have been much use to me. You yourself dont know whether my plays will be of any use to you when you have found yourself.

Goodnight.   G.B.S.

Ellen Terry, with whom Shaw had a long correspondence, first appeared on the London stage the year Shaw was born; created Dame Ellen in 1925, she was married to the painter G. F. Watts; popular on both sides of the Atlantic, she toured the U. S. on ten separate occasions.

May Morris, daughter of Shaw's friend the medievalist William Morris, was very close to Shaw for many years.

AYOT ST LAWRENCE, WELWYN, HERTS.
STATION: WHEATHAMPSTEAD, G.N.R. 2¼ MILES.
TELEGRAMS: BERNARD SHAW, CODICOTE. 26th November 1922. 10 ADELPHI TERRACE, W.C.2.

My dear Mollytompkins

    I have seldom been more flabbergasted -- if ever -- than when I learnt from your letter that you have not been learning elocution at the R.A.D.A. In Heaven's name, what HAVE you been learning ? Elocution is ninetynine hundredths of what I advised you to go to the School to learn. That it is possible for a student to attend the academy and omit elocution as if it were an extra like freehand drawing or Chinese heiroglyphics comes to me as a staggering absurdity. There must be some technical catch in it which I do not understand ; for you have spoken of learning voice production and all sorts of elocutionary things. But if the omission of what they call elocution in the time sheet of the school disqualifies you from taking a diploma, why were you allowed to omit it ? Before I raise the question with Mr Barnes, I should like some further light on it.

    I was about to advise you to use the spare time given you by the maid's parts (which of course you ought to have taken, even if you "made a face" to express your disgust) to work at French with Mlle Gachet. Nothing is more instructive to a speaker than mastering the pronunciation of a foreign language. So you are on the right line there ; but you had better tell Mlle that you have lost every penny of your money and must now earn your bread and that of your infant son, Lawrence having fallen down an area and broken his back. You may throw in two blind and bedridden grandparents and a destitute mother if you feel in the vein. For I solemnly warn you that if the idea gets about that you are able and willing to finance theatrical ventures for the sake of getting parts, you will be fleeced so thoroughly that you will not know what a new hat is for fifty years. And if you go to agents and put on airs of gaiety (which you will do very badly, thank God !)you will only tempt them to try to get something more than money out of you ; and they are not all proof against that temptation. So put all that nonsense out of your head. Dont forget that every rich woman who is paying for an appearance is making it harder for poor women to get a living wage for their work, and driving them to make the stage just the shop window for business of quite another sort.

As to your troubles at Gower St, they are all due to the fact that
Sarah of Red Gulch has no manners. Sarah always thinks that if what she
says is true, and what she demands is within her rights, it does not matter how she says it or demands it. And Sarah is at her worst when she
starts in to make a scene with a resolution to behave herself with the
strictest self-control and politeness. There is nothing on earth quite
so offensive as politeness to people who are on familiar terms with you.
If you must make rows with Mr Barnes and Mr Rains, for heaven's sake make
them as rowdy as possible : give them some tragi-comic acting : call them
names (especially their Christian names) : accuse them of impossible
crimes and then fall weeping convulsively on their chests : do anything
rather than be acidly polite and insolent. But if I tell you to do these
things there is a horrible danger of your literally trying to do them ;
and I dont think you can act well enough yet to make a success of it. But
if you deliberately tell Mr Rains's principal (NOT principle) in his presence that his preference for more amiable students has a corrupt motive,
which is the very worst thing you can suggest of a teacher in such an institution, what, O unmollifiable Molly, can you expect ?

Mr Tittle has obtained an introduction from Drinkwater. I know nothing of his work : what does Lawrence think of it ? Sitting for portrait
is no fun ; and unless the result is at least better than a photograph
(which it often isnt) the time is wasted.

In great haste -- if you knew how hard it is to
find a moment to write !

Hearing through the R.A.D.A. grapevine that Michael King,
manager of the Plymouth Repertory Theatre, needed a leading
lady for a year's contract and that Kenneth Barnes had the giving
of the job to an R.A.D.A. senior, M.T. cut them all out by
catching a train for Plymouth and talking King into giving her
the job.

10, ADELPHI TERRACE. W.C.2.

1st December 1922.
AYOT ST LAWRENCE, WELWYN, HERTS.
STATION: WHEATHAMPSTEAD, G.N.R. 2¼ MILES.
TELEGRAMS: BERNARD SHAW, CODICOTE.

Dear Mollytompkins

All this is first rate: you couldn't have done better. As far as I can guess without being on the spot the Plymouth Repertory is a gallant little enterprise; and I have always given Mr King the licenses he asked for when my hands were not tied by other contracts.

It is almost a pity that you did not get that contract out of him whilst he was under the first spell of your good looks. Now that he is saner he very properly wants a try-out before he commits himself; but I daresay you will pull it off. But take good care of yourself during the ordeal.

As to the contract, remember that though I advise you to secure a years contract at £15 a week if you can get it I am assuming that there is nothing in the contract that ought not to be in it. For instance, if it obliged you to provide your dresses, it would be impossible. You should join the Actors' Association, and take its advice on the subject. But meanwhile you can ask Mr King for a draft of the contract to shew to your husband before you sign it. It was very straight of him to tell you that you should shew it to your solicitor. So you should — if only solicitors knew anything about the theatre. No harm if you shew it to me.

Write immediately and joyously to Mr Barnes to say that you can't play on the 11th (don't leave it an open question in any way). Ask him to forgive you for stealing the engagement, and say that you are wild with delight and will ever regard him as the founder of your fortunes. Send your love to Mr Rams if you like.

It is frightfully unlucky about the flat & the studio; but such things are still so much in demand that you should be able to trade them off again and settle in Plymouth for the year. Except for fashionable portrait work the sea air is ever so much better for sculpture. Let me know how you got on: I always have time to read letters; and if I haven't time to answer them, why, I haven't, and that's all.

G.B.S.

P.S. Lawrence wrote me a very pertinent letter about Little: just what I wanted.

AYOT ST LAWRENCE, WELWYN, HERTS.
STATION: WHEATHAMPSTEAD, G.N.R. 2¼ MILES.   10th December 1922.   10 ADELPHI TERRACE.W.C.2.
TELEGRAMS: BERNARD SHAW, CODICOTE.

Dear Mollytompkins

There are two ways of getting across the footlights. One is to shout the play into the audience so that they can't attend to anything else. The other, Mrs Patrick Campbell's way, is to make the audience come across to her and listen to her. This requires not only fascination but the art of speaking so as to be heard and understood without effort : that is, very precise and detailed articulation, so that, whilst the actress is utterly ignoring the audience (or seeming to) she is really taking the greatest care that no essential word or group of words is lost on them. It is rarer and more difficult than the shouting ; but when everybody else is shouting it is the only way to get distinction.

Do not, however, imagine that the vigorous speech that is needed for public purposes is shouting because at first it seems more violent than ordinary conversation. Real shouting is no use : it does not travel ; and it worries the audience. As far as mere loudness goes, never go to the utmost of your power : always keep well inside it. It is articulation that tells. If you are particular about that ; and keep your tone agreeable, you will be heard. The only remaining difficulty is the great art of choosing the key words on which the sentence depends for its intelligibility, and stressing them. You may articulate as perfectly as you please, and yet be inexpressive and even quite unintelligible. It may sound like the alphabet and nothing else. For instance :

Whatifitbeapoisonwhichthefriarsubtlyhathministeredtohavemedead ?

You may articulate that beautifully and produce the finest tone on every vowel and yet it will mean nothing, especially if it is all on one note.

Whatt iff itt umum Poison ! umum frrriar
Umum um umumum ttoo hhavvv meee dddeaddd ?

That will be perfectly intelligible and effective. Get out the words from which the audience can guess the rest ; and the others will take care of themselves : they are useful only for rhythm.

For Mrs. Patrick Campbell, one of the great figures of the English stage, Shaw wrote the part of Eliza in *Pygmalion*, which she played in the first London production in 1914. To Forbes-Robertson's Romeo and Hamlet she played Juliet and Ophelia. With Shaw, who called her "perilously bewitching," she maintained a long correspondence, published after her death in 1940 with a preface by Shaw.

30

When the language is poetic instead of colloquial, you must take great care of the words that are not used in ordinary conversation, because the audience cannot guess them and will not take the meaning in so quickly as when you are giving them common idiomatic phrases. If you say

Woff terangelsthrough thisguise, Fa rabove yonazh erplane

you might as well say it in Chinese. You must say Waftt hher, no matter how pedantic it sounds. But it wont sound pedantic to the audience unless you articulate ssounds that are spelt but never spoken. If you call angels Ain Jells, so as to rhyme to bluebells, or organ Orr Gann,rhyming to dustpan, it will sound ridiculous. What is called "the Obscure Vowel" (the second one in butter) plays a great part in English and has no letter in the alphabet to indicate it : sometimes it is o, sometimes u, sometimes ou, sometimes a , and the phoneticians indicate it by e turned upside down. The Irish and some Americans read i as an obscure vowel and say merrut and spirrutwhilst the English say very distinctly merit and spirit ; so be careful.

But you should practice all this until it becomes completely automatib; for there is nothing more annoying than an actress or a singer who is thinking about her technique when she ought to be thinking only of the sense and feeling of her part. Her voice simply wonnk won't modulate. In the end one becomes so expert in both ways that one can live on the two planes simultaneously, and in the middle of a transport of dramatic passion remember that such and such a word is difficult to hear, and give it a special articulation accordingly.

I give you all this lecturing because I think your best plan may be to be quiet, cool, aloof, enigmatic, and quite unlike the rest : and for that a good technique of speech is very important, as nothing is of any use unless the audience can hear every word without effort.

You should flatly refuse to sign that contract unless Mr King undertakes to provide your dresses. It is usual and proper that he should, as no actress could possibly afford to dress on such a salary : it means for you only trenching on your private means ; but for other women it means prostitution. Dont be afraid to put your foot down on this point : he knows very well that he should dress you. As a matter of fact he will do it so poorly that you will probably have to supplement his efforts ; but he will have to

(3)

contribute

something ; and you will have done your duty to your profession.

In plays like Jane, it is useless to expect any success except the success of the piece as a farcical comedy of a not very refined sort. ~~they~~ will be mere drudgery ; but perhaps you had better dance through them than sit them out.

As people die in Plymouth occasionally they must have tombstones made on the spot (unless they order them from the Stores) : and I believe Lawrence could pick up a staff on the spot to do his pointing and all the rest of it. Or, like Michael Angelo, he might do it all with the chisel himself.

Or why shouldnt he work in wood -- a delightful art -- and make figureheads for the coasting schooners, half of which are called The Molly. He could fill in with Virgin Maries for the Roman Catholic churches, having so excellent a model to his hand. A steady trade of that kind is much better than gentleman like Art.

Let me know how you get on when you are not too tired to write.

PS Why dont you boldly call yourself Molly Tompkins professionally? It is a capital name for 3 reasons. 1. It is very memorable. 2. Nobody else would dream of taking it. 3. It is your real name. Mary Arthur is characterless: there is no bite in it: it is schoolgirlish. Remember, you have to choose a name most carefully and build it up from the beginning. After the first playbill; it will be too late to change. Molly Tompkins is a challenge — a gesture. Try it.

The Postscript reads:

P.S. Why dont you boldly call yourself Molly Tompkins professionally? It is a capital name for 3 reasons. 1. It is very *memorable*. 2. Nobody else would dream of taking it. 3. It is your real name. Mary Arthur is characterless: there is no bite in it: it is schoolgirlish. Remember, you have to choose a name most carefully and build it up from the beginning. After the first playbill, it will be too late to change. Molly Tompkins is a challenge—a gesture. Try it.

AYOT ST LAWRENCE, WELWYN, HERTS.
STATION: WHEATHAMPSTEAD, G.N.R.2¼ MILES.
TELEGRAMS: BERNARD SHAW, CODICOTE.

22nd December 1922.

IO ADELPHI TERRACE.W.C.2.

My dear Mollytompkins

Shingles, a ridiculous but distressing complaint, usually follows prolonged worry culminating in a fearful temper tantrum. Did you lose your temper ? And are you well now ?

I have been giving you warnings about your vowels and consonants when I should have been giving you warnings about your meals. At Godalming you had barely enough to eat at the regular meals ; and yet you could never eat them, and were always emptying your plate into the interior of the starving Lawrence. That was not wifely devotion : it was a surfeit of chocolate creams and things. The woman who never eats is always eating. She never gives her unfortunate digestion an off time ; and it very soon goes wrong and takes its revenge on her complexion and on her figure. I exhort you (in the manner of Higgins) to remember that you are a human being with a soul and the divine gift of articulate speech, and not a confectioner's shop. Bundle these silly people out of your dressing room with their nips and snacks : they had much better suck their thumbs like the babies they are. Some of them will end by taking cocktails and keeping up the supply of the drink tragedies of the stage. I am fond of sweets, like most teetotallers ; but I eat three times a day only ; and I am convinced that three times is once too often.

It is really very difficult to know exactly how an actress should pamper herself without ruining her health. She needs pampering or she would very soon have no more charm than I have ; but however wildly extravagant she may be in everything else, she should not be extravagant in eating and drinking. Daniel became beautiful by vegetarianism (at least the Bible says so) but he probably let himself go on gold backed hairbrushes and costly robes. Also she must not love anyone or give any kisses that are not stage kisses. She can, however, make others love her ; so that when her extravagance has ruined her she can extricate herself by publishing their love letters.

This reminds me of Henry, of whom I never heard before. It relieves me of an occasional anxiety to learn that there is somebody looking after you two who knows something about business.

The danger of telling you anything is startlingly illustrated by your proposals to obtain a good handwriting by going to a school where a good commercial hand can be acquired at a reasonable fee. There used to be a place

if I had explained that your handwriting is illegible, which it is not in the least.

The note reads:

. . . as if I had explained that your handwriting is
illegible, which it is not in the least.

at the top of Pentonville Hill where they taught copperplate with flourishes. And you think that that is what Higgins taught Eliza! You just wait until I give you more precise instructions. I shall write to May Morris, and ask her where she found the models on which she formed her lovely handwriting. William Morris worked a bit at caligraphy and turned out some manuscripts which are presentable, though of course they count for nothing beside his poetry and printing and designing. I did get a book for you ; but it would have confused you ; so I witheld it. I enclose a Christmas card with a ⬛⬛⬛ specimen of a very offhand artistic hand. *It is undistinguished and slapdash; but it has artistic intentions*

My own handwriting was not natural to me : I acquired it for the purpose of keeping a cashbook neatly in my teens, when I was a slave in an office.

Before learning to write beautifully, acquire the art of saying No in a convincing manner. It is the most useful accomplishment in the world ; and your life will be a long misery unless you can bring it out swiftly and unanswerably without the slightest regard to the feelings or the importance of the petitioner or autocrat or whoever it is who asks or orders you to do something you dont want to do. Will you have a drink ? NO. Will you lend me two pounds until Saturday night when I will -- NO. Will you sign a contract to dress yourself on £5 a week ? NO. Will you accept this little rope of pearls, and come with me in my Rolls Royce from Sunday morning to Monday afternoon ? NO. May I introduce you to a gentleman who is particularly anxious to -- NO. Will you give me an introduction to Bernard Shaw as I think he might give me a part in his next play ? NO. Do you call yourself a lady ? NO : get out.

Penlee is only a villa on the road to Slapton, not worth stopping at. Drive right on to Slapton Sands, two miles between the fresh water and the salt, to the hotel, which is full of memories for me. I made my will there once ; and Lillah McCarthy witnessed it, with Dion Clayton Calthrop, Granville Barker, Violet Asquith (Lady Bonham Carter) and all sorts of people .

I rejoice to hear that you collared your audience after a night or two. The road is now open before you. Let me know how you get on.

The note reads:

It is undistinguished and slapdash; but it has artistic intentions.

Henry is Laurence's elder brother, Henry B. Tompkins of Atlanta, Georgia, president of the Robinson-Humphrey Co.

Lillah McCarthy, English actress who first appeared in Drinkwater's company in the 1890s. Granville-Barker, English actor, producer, dramatist, critic. Dion Clayton Calthrop, dramatic author and designer, son of Eve Boucicault.

34

The card reads:

People who have any positive character always begin in that cold way; but they go farthest in the end. The emotional spooks succeed almost at once but do not improve with age. Lady T. is a very tricky part for a comedian. It requires some experience to overdo it in the conventional way and play Sir Peter off the stage; but I prefer the play with Sir P. as the star; and I never could endure Lady T's dishonorable sacrifice of poor Joseph in the last act (a man would be kicked for it); nor does the fun of Charles quite get over his blackguardism. I really think that I should cast you for Maria . . . I remember a famous prima donna, Tietjens, who used to bow before the curtain with such expansive friendliness that a clergyman once rose in the pit and returned the bow. Think of those hard earned shillings, spent to

(over)

(continuation on back of card)

forget the hardness of life for a few hours, and to believe romantic things about you! How can you be cold or unkind to them? Do you realize how poor most of them are? Irving was at his best before the curtain: always "your faithful servant", and consequently "the greatest among you". When you get the right feeling about them it will all come right; and you will be their darling.

G.B.S.

Sir Peter and Lady Teazle, the main characters in Sheridan's *The School for Scandal*. M.T. was supposed to twist and twirl, be coy and twitter, laugh and be mischievous: hence her coldness.

IO ADELPHI TERRACE
LONDON W.C.2.

March 1st 1923.

Dear Mollytompkins,

Consider that I have written you half a dozen letters.
I meant them, but hadn't time to put them on paper. I met Lawrence and told him to explain to you that you were getting clergyman's sore throat by pitching your voice too low.

An actress is not constituted: she grows. Why, exactly,
has Mr King given you the sack? Of course you could not deliver
the goods; but he can hardly have expected you to do more than
you should have been able to do.

Anyhow you are getting on quite satisfactorily by the
usual rather painful process of shedding your illusions. First,
you think you are through with me; and though you are not, yet
it is a great advance to be able to think so. Second, you now
say what I have so often pointed out to you: that a passion for
my plays has nothing whatever to do with the power (mainly mus-
cular) of sending them across the footlights.

Did you offer to manage the theatre for Mr King? You
may be too clever to be an actress. You have some taste; and you
write well in your barbarous way that your letters always enter-
tain me quite apart from Molly.

I don't think that you are unhappy or doubt that you
are all right; but I will write to you if I like: so there!

                    Ever,
                    G. Bernard Shaw.

Mrs Lawrence Tompkins,
1a Lugham Street,
Plymouth.

10. ADELPHI TERRACE. W.C.2.

13th March 1923.

AYOT ST LAWRENCE, WELWYN, HERTS.
STATION: WHEATHAMPSTEAD, G.N.R. 2¼ MILES.
TELEGRAMS: BERNARD SHAW, CODICOTE.

Dear Mollytompkins

I know nothing about these people : some of them are very decent : others are blackguards. You must ask the Actors Association (I presume you are a member : you ought to be) : they know the black sheep pretty well.

If you have never heard of Vedrenne & Barker (Granville Barker), and the Shavian boom at the Court Theatre from 1904 on under their management, you have never heard of anything. You should read Desmond McCarthy's book about it. I will tell you about Vd when next we meet.

I write in great haste — I have not a moment.

G.B.S.

Fired from the Plymouth Repertory Theatre, M.T. decided that the only cure was to stand once more on the boards; in her dealings with all sorts of managers she asked Shaw for information and advice; among those she encountered were Vedrenne and Barker, who as managers of the Court Theatre first made a success of Shaw in London. Desmond MacCarthy, London drama and literary critic, knighted in 1951, wrote a book on the Court Theatre 1904—7.

AYOT ST LAWRENCE, WELWYN, HERTS. 20ᵗʰ March 1923   10, ADELPHI TERRACE. W.C.2.
STATION: WHEATHAMPSTEAD, G.N.R. 2¼ MILES
TELEGRAMS: BERNARD SHAW, CODICOTE.

Don't you dare start preaching at me, Mollytompkins. You just do what I tell you.

By a blackguard manager I do not mean anything that you can defend yourself against. But there are desperadoes who take companies out knowing quite well that unless they take money enough at the doors to pay the salaries the unfortunate troupe will be left stranded, penniless and in debt, perhaps 300 miles from their homes. There are rascals who, if they make a good haul at the pay boxes, simply bolt with it, with the same result. The Actors' Association has to hunt down these fellows; and so it comes to know them, and also, of course, to know the regular touring managers who can be depended on. That is why I told

you to consult the A.A. before engaging
with anyone you dont know.

The manager who tours with my plays
is Charles Macdona, of Faraday House,
8-10 Charing † Road W.C.2. I think I
recollect your agony at witnessing one of his
productions. But Charles is as respectable as
the Bank of England; and some of his
professional competitors are as much the reverse
as it is possible for human beings to be.

So take care whom you go out with.

By immemorial stage tradition a manager is entitled to address all the females in his company as darling, and all the males as 'old boy'. It has been falling into disuse of late; but I sometimes resort to it myself when a leading lady is exasperatingly inattentive and keeps the stage waiting whilst she is chatting with somebody instead of minding her business. Its use seldom implies sincere affection.

Mouldy Mike writes asking may he put on The Doctor's Dilemma & Major Barbara.

At the annual performance of the R.A.D.A., Betty Pollock introduced a rather attractive lady whose name I did not catch, saying she wanted to speak to

26th March 1923. AYOT ST LAWRENCE, WELWYN, HERTS. STATION: WHEATHAMPSTEAD, G.N.R. 2¼ MILES. TELEGRAMS: BERNARD SHAW, CODICOTE

M. T. was signed by a Mr. Norris to go on the road as the lead in Oscar Wilde's *A Woman of No Importance*. Mouldy Mike was the familiar name by which everyone referred to Michael King of the Plymouth Repertory Theatre.

me. I shook hands with her in my most gracious manner. To my surprise she immediately bolted as if Betty had played a trick on her. I thought no more of it until Mr. Lang, who was looking on, said "Wasn't that your Molytonphis?" Then the lady's face came back to me with your eyes and front hair, and staggered me for a moment, into asking myself could Plymouth have transmogrified you to such an extent that you had taken me in. However, I dismissed that possibility, especially as Mr. Lang is firmly persuaded that I am never absent from your side for a moment except when I am under her direct observation. You made a terrific impression on her very vivid imagination.

In great haste

Betty Pollock, an English actress the same age as M. T., was playing on the London stage that season.

TELEGRAMS:
"METROPOLE, MINEHEAD."
TELEPHONE No. 11.

5th April 1923.

Hotel Metropole.

Minehead, Somerset.

I think you will have to begin making experiments with your own way of doing things. You need not take the bit between your teeth at once all the time; but you might claim a night for yourself — say Tuesday or Friday — or an act for yourself, or, to begin, a speech or two for yourself, and see whether they do not go as well as in the coached way. There is only one way of getting your own way; and that is making your own way convincing in action. It is quite possible that your notion of doing the thing is the right notion, but that you have not yet got skill enough to put it across; and so for the moment you must do as the others do; but in the end you must make yourself something more than a marionette worked mostly by somebody who is not a successful actor or author or critic or connoisseur or anything else that commands an unquestioning deference.

I do not gather from your undated letter whether you are going on with Mr Norris: in fact I am not clear as to whether he is on tour or a fixture in Salisbury. Also I dont know what "next week" means, as your letter had to follow me here and I dont know when you wrote it.

I am here at the mudside (the Bristol channel can hardly be called sea) to recuperate for a week or two if we can stand it. We shall potter about in the old car until we go to Stratford on the 30th.

I cannot write a decent sentence; and I wish the sun would come out.

TELEGRAMS:
"METROPOLE, MINEHEAD."
TELEPHONE No. 11.

8th April 1923

Hotel Metropole,

Minehead, Somerset.

I ought not to shew you this; and you must never let him know that you have seen it (but it up now); but on the whole you'd better. You should go on until you have learnt the trade, so that you may have a trade and not be just an odalisque; for what use is an odalisque after thirty? You need not bother about your top register: Sarah Bernhardt played all her parts on her top register; and though I loathed her intoning and whining the critics accepted it as a *voix d'or*.

She actually rehearsed her death for the movies to pay for her funeral: I saw the film in Bath, and was amazed.

Remember that in the theatre you must cut yourself loose completely and remorselessly at every remove. Otherwise you will sink like a ship crusted with barnacles. Plymouth is dead: long live Salisbury!

Besides, managers are always on the brink of ruin; and actors are always going out into the pit.

Enclosed was Michael King's letter explaining why he had fired M.T. from the Plymouth Repertory, saying that her voice was always or almost always on top register.

THE MALVERN HOTEL,
MALVERN. 27th Ap. 1923

Dear Mollytompkins

The enclosed (which tear up) may interest you.

You cannot set up a theatre with a capital of £200 & two partners. The unpardoneable crime — the crime of the bogus manager — is to start without enough money to pay a fortnights salaries and retire with honor in the event of a failure.

Do not let anybody get money out of you. The text "Where the carcass is there will the eagles be gathered together" clearly refers to the stage. Dont be the carcass.

Who is V ? A frightful liar, if she says she has managed companies for years and can go into management afresh if you give her £100. Dont .

I am beginning a new play . after all —
another historical one .

[signature]

V. referred to a certain woman.

The new play is *Saint Joan,* though M.T.
says that they were at Stratford-on-Avon when
Shaw first announced that he was going to
write about Joan of Arc "to save her from
Drinkwater!"

46

Please explain to any idiot who may bewail to you my devotion to Macdona that he has now been a steady source of income to me for 12 years; that he keeps a company touring through the provinces with my plays exclusively; that he monopolizes only about half a dozen of them, leaving plenty for others; that he can hardly be expected to bring a play to a provincial city only to find that some local company has just squeezed it dry; and that the result of free competition in my plays would be the ruin of all the competitors and finally of the author. The people who do not understand this and accept it as a necessary part of theatrical business are amateurs, or novices, or inexperienced geese like Mollytompkins.

Your Court friend, by the way, was up against Macdermott, not Macdona; but the situation is the same: the Court would ruin the Everyman; and the Everyman would ruin the Court. G.B.S

AYOT ST LAWRENCE, WELWYN, HERTS. 28th May 1929. 10, ADELPHI TERRACE. W.C.2.
STATION: WHEATHAMPSTEAD, G.N.R. 2¼ MILES.
TELEGRAMS: BERNARD SHAW, CODICOTE.

The last two lines read:

...is the same: the Court would ruin the Everyman; and the Everyman would ruin the Court.

G.B.S.

Charles Macdona, Irish actor turned manager, organized the Macdona Players, who took Shaw's plays on tour, not only in England and Ireland, but Europe, Africa, India, and the Far East. Norman Macdermott, producer and director, founder of the Everyman's Theatre in Hampstead, reintroduced Shaw's plays to the London stage after years of neglect, producing eight in a series of "Shaw Seasons" after the war.

Eccles Hotel. Glengarriff. Co. Cork, 4/8/23

Dear Mollytompkins

Yesterday I suddenly thought "What has become of Molly?" not having had the subject before me for ages. This morning I see your name in The Times as one of Lion's Liverpool company, and receive your letter. Telepathy is evidently not instantaneous; but it is faster than the post to Ireland.

The Times announcement settles the question of the name for ever. Even in the Times paragraph the extraordinary effectiveness of Molly Tompkins comes out. I considered the matter very carefully before I advised you to use it. I do not know who the gentleman is who is pursuing you with suggestions of Evadne Evremond and the like. If he has shown in his own career a greater knowledge of how to achieve success than I, you will prefer his advice. If not you will perhaps tell him that you are acting by my advice. This will give you his measure exactly enough for all your purposes. If he has any sense he will shut up like an alarmed oyster, and tell everyone that *he* told you to stick to your own name. If he is the common fool of the theatre he will assure you that "Shaw was laughing at you or did it just to make game of you. You mustn't take him seriously."

I rely on you not to give a second thought to the advice of anyone who talks like that. A malicious fool thinks everyone else a malicious fool. Beware of such fools. And do not forget that I warned you that the theatre is fuller than most places of failures who are always imparting the secret of success to those who are inexperienced enough to listen to them, and of mediocrities (technically knows as "utilities") offering advice which is quite sound for themselves, but disastrous for more gifted people.

Besides the people who give advice, there are the people who take it. Everybody who is not quite unapproachable gets a mixed lot of advice, good and bad. The people who are no good *select* the bad advice, and dare not take the good. That is why it is so useless to try to help people whom God does not mean to be helped. If Shakespear tells them what to do, and their dresser tells them to do the opposite, they will do the opposite, just as they will buy racing tips from some shabby desperado who would obviously be a millionaire if he were a judge of horses.

You were very lucky to get this engagement with Lion: and I hope you will make good. Anyhow, the experience will be valuable.

Lawrence is quite right in making you tell me about your movements, but his advice has not saved you from incivility. Nothing could be more uncivil than to fling the news at me and say you suppose it doesn't interest me. You are still a frightful young cub in spite of your refined appearance and your Georgian traditions. However, you will grow out of it, unless success spoils you.

Mildewed Mike has produced Brassbound. I have just had his cheque for the fees. Methuselah will be produced at Birmingham: I may have to go there for some of the rehearsals. Between that and Heartbreak House at Oxford I do not expect to return home until late in October.

For the moment I am here, but may move on further west. However, the address is safe for a week or so.

G.B.S.

48

Parknasilla. Kenmare. Co. Kerry. 27th Aug. 1923

My dear Molly

£5 is all right. A woman can live on it if she has not to find her dresses; and as long as you do not drive salaries below subsistence point, which means compulsory prostitution for competitors who have no private means, you can take as little as you please. £5 used to be the salary of a leading lady in a touring melodrama. £3 is, I think, the minimum wage of the Actors' Association; but it is not enough for a speaking part and some personal beauty.

It is no use Mr Vachell asking you to get laughs. You are not a comedian, alias soubrette, alias "singing chambermaid": your aspect is tragic; and you must tell them flatly that it can't be done: you have not a laughcatching note in your voice, and must succeed for the present as a woman of sorrows, with eyes like muscatel grapes, drowning the stage with washed tears instead of setting the table in a roar.

I know the Midland Adelphi very well, and its telephones which nobody ever answers. But its bathrooms — one for each room — are enlarged to a degree very exceptional in England; so be thankful.

It is a great gift to be able to endure and enjoy solitude. Handel was like that; so it may be a sign of greatness. People who can't bear to be alone for a moment are never great, unless they are afraid of ghosts.

It is also very prudent to be fascinated and maddened by old men with wives and a lot of work to do, as the poor old creatures like it and are harmless.

The weather has been so wet here lately that I have worked like a Trojan. Saint Joan is finished (except for the polishing) : a magnificent play; — and I thought I should never write another after Methuselah ! I am certainly a wonderful man ; but then historical plays hardly count : the material is readymade.

Horace Annesley Vachell, dramatist and author, born 1861, was the author of *Blinkers*. Elizabeth Irving, twenty-year-old daughter of Henry Irving, was to play the lead; M.T. the part of a society woman. On the road they became good friends.

I intend at present to stay here until the middle of September, having given up the Fabian Summer School. Then I shall make for Birmingham, to look after Methuselah.

Let me know how you get on. C. V. France played Morell in Candida for me about 20 years ago. I have never seen Elizabeth: she has a very clever mother, and between that and a fascinating father she ought to be well stocked hereditarily.

ever

C. V. France was one of the leads in *Blinkers* who expressed doubt about the play's chances of success in London.

Parknasilla. Kenmare. Co. Kerry. 28/5/23

Yes, yes, yes; but what is it all about? Clairvoyance is not one of my gifts.

No: I never look at a play after the first night, and wouldn't look at it then (Pinero never does) if I didn't think my absence would seem impolite to the company after all their work for me. No play was ever saved by tinkering, or ever will be. G.B.S.

Miss Molly Tompkins
Caledonian Hotel
Edinburgh

Scotland.

M.T. had asked Shaw to attend the opening night of *Blinkers*.

Parknasilla (last day but one) 12th Sept. 1923
NEXT WEEK The Malvern Hotel. Great Malvern. Worcs.

Your letters are very amusing, dear Molly; but they should be dated, and, when you are on tour, headed with next week's address as above.

Blinkers would appear to be doomed. It is a bad sign when an author tinkers his play after production; but it is absolutely decisive when the actor-manager drops his part and hands it over to another actor. In his opinion at any rate a fatal result is certain; so you had better all be prepared for your fortnights notices. I am sorry, not only for your sake, but generally, because every failure hurts the theatre at large and everyone connected with it.

It may be, however, that the cast is wrong.

I have not noticed that you are so very different to anyone else, including myself. You have the usual number of eyes, ears, fingers and toes. The tiny trifle that distinguishes Molly Tompkins from Polly Perkins is only a fraction of the entire Molly. Taken in the lump they have the same needs, passions, curiosities, delusions, &c. &c. &c. &c. The tiny trifle needs a lot of cultivation before it becomes significant and thrillingly distinctive. I shouldn't worry about it.

The day after tomorrow (Friday the 14th) I cross back to England, and after a couple of days wandering pull up for a while at Malvern as above. Methuselah will be produced on the 9th October in Birmingham; but I have settled nothing yet as to my movements in relation to the rehearsals.

Saint Joan is finished, except for revision and arrangement of the stage business.

In haste—it is very difficult to find a moment to write

G.B.S.

Shaw was right about *Blinkers:* well received in Liverpool and panned in Edinburgh, it ran one week at the Savoy in London.

MALVERN HOTEL,
MALVERN.
26ᵗʰ Sept. 1923

TELEPHONE NO: 338
TELEGRAMS: MALVERN
MALVERN HOTEL, MALVERN

Iˢᵗ I shall be staying from the
Iˢᵗ to the 13ᵗʰ October at the house
of Barry Jackson, the proprietor
of the Birmingham Repertory Theatre
which is producing Methuselah on the
9ᵗʰ. His address is

53 Wake Green Road
Moseley
Birmingham.

Did I tell you that I broke my
ribs in Ireland on the rocks, and am
a wreck as far as my bones are concerned?

G. Bernard Shaw.

Mʳˢ Lawrence Tompkins
42 Chepstow Villas
W. 11.

1st October 1923

TEL. 289, SOUTH.

53, WAKE GREEN ROAD,
MOSELEY,
BIRMINGHAM.

Dear Mollytompkins

I suppose I ought not to shew you the enclosed letter; but I have to explain to you something that has happened. Armstrong wrote to me to say that he had rashly promised you Lavinia in Androcles, and wanted to know whether I thought you could play it As I haven't seen you act since Gower St, I really couldn't honestly guarantee you as fully competent for a leading part of such importance. Fortunately the enclosed letter enabled me to reply by return to Armstrong that F.R. had seen you act lately, and had spoken of you in such extraordinarily eulogistic terms that he could ask no better testimonial, and ought to jump at you. And I hope he will.

The letter will fill you up enough to leave no room for one of mine, which is lucky, as my damaged ribs make most activities painful for the present.

I shall be here until the 13th. This is the house of Barry Jackson, the proprietor & manager of the Repertory Theatre here

ever

G.B.S.

The enclosed letter was from Forbes-Robertson to Shaw. William Armstrong, an actor born in Edinburgh, who had just become director of the Liverpool Repertory Theatre, had seen M.T. in *Blinkers* and wanted her for Lavinia in *Androcles and the Lion*.

TEL. 289, SOUTH.

1st October 1923.

53, WAKE GREEN ROAD,
MOSELEY,
BIRMINGHAM.

c/o Barry Jackson

My dear Forbes-Robertson

Your letter was not only very welcome to me but very useful to Molly. I have not seen her attempt to act since she was a student at Gower St. Consequently I was in a difficulty when William Armstrong, of the Liverpool Repertory Theatre, who had been led away by her good looks into offering her the leading part in a production of Androcles & The Lion, became conscious that he had acted in an infatuated manner, and wrote to me to ask me whether I really thought she could play it. I was about to reply reluctantly but honestly that I could not answer for her hard professional competence, as I had not seen her act since she had been a little through the mill, when your letter came and took my breath away. I wrote to Armstrong at once saying that you had spoken of her acting and her attraction in such terms that, far from hesitating, he should just jump at her. I hope the result will be that she will appear in Liverpool as Lavinia. I presume her present suspended engagement will not come to anything, as it is evident that the play is a failure. If Lavinia comes off happily she will owe her chance to you. It is very kind of you to encourage her. She could get no higher testimonial; and she needs one, because I have done nothing but sit on her. She has gorgeous nights of happiness when you take her to the theatre. They need some nursing, those two innocent infants. I thought at one time that she was likely to succeed as a writer rather than as an actress, because her descriptive letters are very vivid; and she has an eye for character.

By the way, when I say that your letter took away my breath, I should add that I had hardly any left just then. The day before you wrote it I was on a slab of sloping granite, ice polished, on the Kerry coast, when my heels flew up and I did the back fall of my life. Unluckily I had a camera about as large (in its case) as a brick, slung on my back; and it was driven almost through me under my left shoulder. I was so completely knocked out that I thought, as I sprawled there, that my ribs, lungs, heart and kidney were all in a mash. The doctors within reach said nothing was broken, but I was bruised and should be black & blue next day. I had to keep going for 12 days before I got into the hands of a properly qualified osteopath and within reach of an X ray apparatus. I was not black & blue; but I cracked my tenth rib and tore it a good deal out of its place; and damaged the ninth also. It took the osteopath about an hour's vigorous wrestling to get my skeleton properly articulated again; and the rib seems to be knitting satisfactorily in spite of my 67 years. There is good hope that in a month or so I shall recover my full range of action and be able to sneeze and lie on my side without hideous twinges.

I tell you this revolting tale to explain why your letter has remained so long unanswered.

I have finished my play "Saint Joan" (of Arc), with one woman's part and 20 men. Would you come back and play Cauchon (rehabilitated) if you were asked by Sybil Thorndike, who is to be Joan? I fear that Gertrude is having a great success

in Australia; and that our deputation to the Treasury has turned out a success.

P.S. As to my business here in Birmingham, see small bill enclosed,

over

G. Bernard Shaw

11th Jan. 1924
10 ADELPHI TERRACE.W.C.2.

Yes, Mollikins; but what _is_ the job? You quite forgot to tell me that.

I _did_ ask L.M.L. about you all right.

I thought you had dropped me in your disillusion and disgust at my publicity stunt at Birmingham. That is the worst of being old: our hardened ways are always blasting the dreams of the young.

Someday you will achieve perfect self-possession, and act simplicity and naturalness to perfection. It will be very agreeable; but it wont be as natural, in your sense, as the heroine of Red Gulch. Sarah may humiliate

The job was a contract for parts in three more plays to be produced in London by Leon M. Lion: the first was to be *Lord o' Creation,* by Norman Macowan, in which M.T. played the part of Lady Esther Pringle.

you, and occasionally injure you; but she doesn't hurt me. I have been through worse places than the Red Gulch myself.

At your age I was frightfully shy, and couldn't please myself, no matter what I did. Learning to live is like learning to skate: you begin by making a ridiculous spectacle of yourself. But the skaters have all been through it. Perhaps that makes their indulgence more exasperating, because it implies that they think you are just like them — an intolerable disparagement to anyone with a starry destiny; so I apologize for even suggesting it.

ever

PS Lawrence's two men be blowed! I'm twenty men at least.

AYOT ST LAWRENCE, WELWYN, HERTS.
STATION: WHEATHAMPSTEAD, G.N.R. 2¼ MILES.   10th February 1924.   IO ADELPHI TERRACE. W.C.2.
TELEGRAMS: BERNARD SHAW, CODICOTE.

My dear Mollytompkins

NOW you know why this particular elderly gentleman bore in mind the maxim of La Rochefoucauld :"The very old and the very young should not speak of love : it makes them ridiculous". Not that I mind being ridiculous any more than Grock does ; but I dont like to give young women cold shivers even when they are good enough to conceal the feelings you so energetically express about certain other gentlemen of my age. A clever young woman has to choose between stupid and vigorous young men and clever and -- shall I say goatish old ones ? See Misalliance passim. But do not be too hard on the poor old things. When David was too old to be interesting to the Bath-shebas he had to turn to the Shunamite woman, who was too young not to be flattered into getting over her disgust.

There are other sets in London than the one you are tired of. All the woman are not mauvaise langues; all the old men were once young ; and there are as good fish in the sea as ever came out of it. There are still revo-lutionary coteries and artistic coteries and musical coteries in which life is youthful and glorious, even to the extent of not washing itself so care-fully as it might. Lawrence can easily break into the artistic ones. You need a social change.

The clinching reason why I can't go on Tuesday night is that I am re-hearsing Methuselah at the Court day and night. But you have to consider, too, that nothing can make a first night as thrilling to me as it is to you and to Lion. For some years I had to go to every first night to earn my bread as a critic. Now I never go on a first night when I can possibly help it : the professional playgoer and the deadhead poison the atmosphere for me. And the theatre is a workshop for me, not a fairyland. If the play runs until my rehearsals are over I will peep in at you some day.

I do not know whether you should stick to acting or not : I have told you before that your talent may be literary, and that acting may be for you only a training and an experience. I feel quite sure that you are cold and a stick as yet, because people with positive characters, like you, have a long struggle with their natural reserve and critical power, whilst others, with no character at all, and very little sense, find selves in plays at once, and exist only when they are on the stage. But the ones with the

positive chracters, who are selves, not spooks, make the best actors when
they go through with it, and are indeed the only possible classical actors.
F.R. is a case in point : he was cold, very handsome, constrained, and with
an air of having been called away from some important business to do something distasteful on the stage. Yet he became our best actor, and indeed is
so still. So there is hope for you if you stick it. Still, a run in Italy
in the spring if this piece fails will do you no harm. It is too hot and
full of mosquitos later on. Mediterranea is a wonderful region : you must
have a bathe in it.
    That, madam, is all for the present, I think.

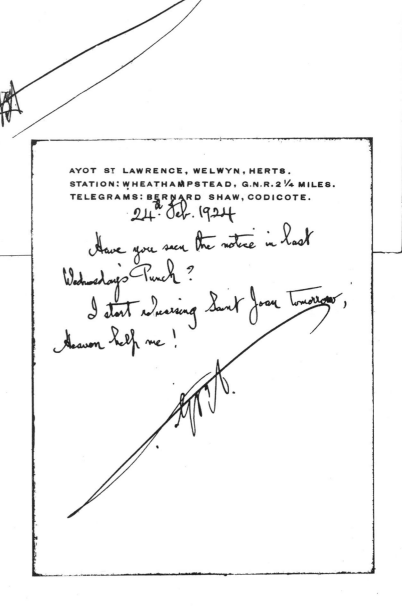

AYOT ST LAWRENCE, WELWYN, HERTS.
STATION: WHEATHAMPSTEAD, G.N.R. 2¼ MILES.
TELEGRAMS: BERNARD SHAW, CODICOTE.

24ᵈ Feb. 1924

Have you seen the notice in last
Wednesday's Punch ?

I start rehearsing Saint Joan tomorrow,
Heaven help me !

The notice in *Punch* appeared next to a
long pan of *Back to Methuselah* and said
simply: "A slight portrait of a drawling
husband-hunting aristocrat was pleasantly
touched in by Miss Molly Tompkins."

3rd March 1924

10 ADELPHI TERRACE. W.C.2.

11·30 p.m.

My dear Molly

You have found your stage legs quite firmly; and your voice is very effective and fine in tone. You are worth your salary now: quite an old professional. But your make-up is "dirty", not transparent & pearly, and the rouge too dark and carried back too far all over your temples. That sort of hat and coat (whatever you call it) would suit a cubbish flapper all legs and neck; but on you it is ugly: your neck requires special study.

The play creates a sufficiently interesting theatrical situation; but instead of solving it the author evades it by an unconvincing move which simply undoes the whole play.

They warned me at the box office that L.M.d. was not playing; but it was my only chance of seeing the play this week; so you must tell him that I was much disappointed, but had to take my luck as it came.

I scribble this in great haste, having to write another line before 11·50. I am in London all the time now, rehearsing Joan for the 26th.

ever

[signature]

Shaw took time out from rehearsing *Saint Joan* at the Court to see M. T. in a matinee of *Lord o' Creation* at the Savoy.

10 ADELPHI TERRACE.W.C.2

Dear Mollywollytompkins:

I wish you as pleasant a trip as the uncertain nature of travelling allows. When you are very tired or bored or furious at having been cheated, remember that travel is for recollections and not for experiences. Also think of M.E.

I cannot give you any tips, because except for a few runs from Biarritz to San Sebastian, and one run up to the Alhambra from Malaga and back (which gave me the brigand scene in Man & Superman) I have never been in Spain. Pronounce all the words with a lisp and remember that gi and ge are H (Algeciras is Al hay theeras and Barcelona Bar-thay--lawna) and you will make a step towards intelligibility. Gib. is Hee-bral-tar.

I did not drill anybody in St Joan. I took more than a thousand notes in my big red note book, all about trifles, and did the drudgery for them; but they were all as free as they wanted to be.

We did that last act of Fanny at the R.A.D.A. show today; and if I had had you for Margaret instead of a young thing who wanted nothing on earth except to be Irene Vanbrugh, it would have been one of the best performances I have ever seen.

Come back soon and tell me all about Spain. I am going to Malvern, Stratford, & Norwich. Shall be back in May — about the 10th, probably.

Poignée de main à Laurent.

G.B.S.

I

If you want to learn Spanish otherwise than by oral instruction, by far the most intelligently arranged course is that of The Palmer Institute, 8 Bloomsbury Mansions, Hart St, W C 1. I forget what it costs: £7 or so, probably; but it is worth it.

But if you contemplate translating plays, remember that you are up against the Granville-Barkers, who

THIS IS A REAL PHOTOGRAPH

CORRESPONDENCE

POST CARD.

ADDRESS

Mr Lawrence
42 Shepherd Villas
London
W. 11.

113   The Bancroft Gardens and Theatre,
From the Tram Bridge, Stratford-on-Avon.

To find a suitably tragic lead for M.T., she and L.T. traveled to Madrid, where Jacinto Benavente put on a special performance of his *La Malquerida* to which he gave them the London rights and asked if they would make a new translation.

II

are fairly formidable rivals. And there are others.

I have a smattering of Spanish, and read your play some time ago, probably when you first mentioned it. Its drawbacks are, from the public point of view, that it is an unhappy story with a horrible ending, and, from your point of view, that the old woman's part is *the* part, and that

THIS IS A REAL PHOTOGRAPH

POST CARD.

CORRESPONDENCE.

ADDRESS

Mrs Laurence Josephus

42 Bhaga

127 Shakespeare's Birthplace, Stratford-on-Avon.

III

anyone who can play it up to concert pitch can wipe you off the stage in your present professional infancy.

Which reminds me, by the way, that you are not within five years hard work of being good enough for Koussevitzky, whose producership I have made a condition of my consent to the Parisian Pygmalion. If it were an American

CORRESPONDENCE.

POST CARD.

ADDRESS.

Mrs Laurence

42 Clapham

London

W. 11.

The Bridges, Stratford-on-Avon

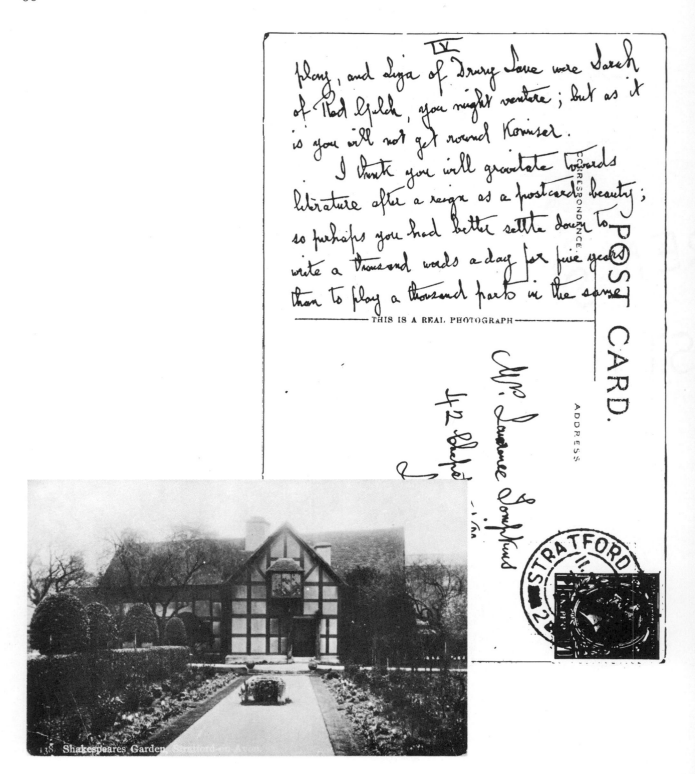

play, and Liza of Drury Lane were Sarah of Red Gulch, you might venture; but as it is you will not get round Komiser.

I think you will gravitate towards literature after a reign as a postcard beauty; so perhaps you had better settle down to write a thousand words a day for five years than to play a thousand parts in the same

THIS IS A REAL PHOTOGRAPH

POST CARD.

CORRESPONDENCE

ADDRESS

Miss Laurence Longland
42 Shaftes

STRATFORD

Shakespeares Garden, Stratford-on-Avon

In London the European producer Theodore Komisarjewski, former director of the Imperial and State theatres in Moscow, was casting for an English *Pygmalion* to be put on in Paris and was considering M.T. for the part of Eliza.

and become a hard hammered actress like Sybil, who can do everything I want with a cock of her eye.

I have just had three hours and a half of Hamlet, and must go to bed. I leave here on Sunday morning, but shall not get home to Ayot until Friday.

THIS IS A REAL PHOTOGRAPH

POST CARD.

CORRESPONDENCE

ADDRESS

Mrs Lawren
42 Glebe
London
W. 11.

The Clopton Bridge, Stratford-on-Avon.

SHAKESPEARE HOTEL.
STRATFORD-ON-AVON.
TELEPHONE 13

30th April 1924

We shall be here until Sunday morning, when I go to Norwich to see a performance of Getting Married and to orate to the local Independent Labor Party — two nights & then home. But it is raining cats and dogs here; and I am slaving all day at my writing table; so your coming might be a sound Shakespearean proposition, but hardly much of a Shavian one.

In future dont shew your letters to Lawrence. Then they wont be torn up, and will probably be much franker. Domestic censorship is always crushing. I will do the tearing-up.

6th May 1924

ROYAL HOTEL,
NORWICH.

Proprietors:
ROYAL HOTEL NORWICH LTD

TELEGRAPHIC ADDRESS:
PRIMUS, NORWICH.

NATIONAL TELEPHONE.
1411, NORWICH.

Molly tompkins : you are an idiot.

This observation is provoked by your proposal to play the old woman in La Malquerida. It is true that Marie O'Neill and her sister played old women wonderfully at the Abbey Theatre in their youth. But it was in the Irish dialect, in a manner native and peculiar, with the support of a whole company playing in the same way after long practice together. That you could perform the same unnatural feat in translated spanish with a scratch London company is wildly improbable. As to doing it with Lawrence's money: well, that will end in his not having any money.

However, the old should not prevent the young making fools of themselves. All I can say is that you have not yet had enough hard and continuous work on the stage to know what you can do, what you can't do, and how to do it. You had much better go and drudge for Mouldy Mike than go on as you are at present: the Spanish trip is all to the good as far as your general culture is concerned; and even your glimpses of London life are not worthless; but as to acting you are not only losing time but going back every night that you are not playing.

As to Eliza, I dont believe you can touch her yet; but if Komisarjevsky thinks you can I shall not interfere. I have said nothing about the cast, and dont intend to. Only, if Komisar lets you get round him — by fair means, no finance — I shall form the lowest opinion of him as a judge.

You are in too great a hurry; and I am in an extremely bad temper, as everything has gone wrong here.

I leave tomorrow morning; so address to Ayot if you write again.

AYOT ST LAWRENCE, WELWYN, HERTS.
STATION: WHEATHAMPSTEAD, G.N.R. 2¼ MILES.
TELEGRAMS: BERNARD SHAW, CODICOTE.

10th June 1924.

IO ADELPHI TERRACE, W.C.2.

My dear Mollytomps

You are quite right : my letters would be ever so much more interesting if they were all about myself instead of being brief instructions to you to keep you out of mischief. You are a delightful correspondent ; and I am a useful bore. But someday I will let you see my autobiographical letters, if I can find any copies of them for the forthcoming collected edition of my works. To write about myself now would be like digging a hole through to Australia : you know not what you ask. Therefore I must confine myself to the statement that my dog's name is Daniel, Marquis of Sealyham, and that the weather seems still uncertain.

Wimbledon is out of the question : I am stuck down here working ; and my mate does not like to be left alone in the domestic cage in the evenings. Besides, I want to see you at work at longer intervals now that you are learning. I am too professionalized to be able to see you in a human way when you are on the stage. It is for the young to sit in ecstasy and wait for you at the stage door at the end, bouquet in hand.

Is it not delightful to be in love ? I will pose for you to your heart's content. You will find it described in Heartbreak House as far as it can be described. It has happened to me twice. It does not last, xxxxx because it does not belong to this earth ; and when you clasp the idol it turns out to be a rag doll like yourself ; for the immortal part must elude you if you grab at it. But it is impossible to write about it : nothing that can be said about it is true. Besides, there is the Song of Solomon, which is still easily the best love poem ever written. When it comes right for a man, then he is in love. When Shelley's Epipsychidion comes right for him, then he only imagines he is in love : he has no notion of the real thing. I wonder is there any poem that comes right for a woman when she is in love. Have you found any ?

But really, Mrs Tompkins, this is hardly a subject --

It is exactly twentyfour hours since I began this letter ; and it will be thirtysix before I finish it -- I mean fortyeight -- unless I break it off. I told you what I thought of that bust when we met at the theatre, and quite put one another out, as happens sometimes. It always upsets me to find myself, helplessly innocent, between you and the other lady, because,

M.T., in a new play by Leon M. Lion based on a novel of Rafael Sabatini, was to try out on the road and she had invited Shaw to attend.

72

though I have not seen either of you for a month, she reproaches me for
having spent that month entirely in your company, and I have an awkward
feeling that you believe I have divided it between her and Ellen, whom I
never see at all.

Why a poor old domesticated drudge, slaving to keep pace with his
work and (worse) his wretched business, should be suspected of being Don
Juan, heaven knows!

Talking of Don Juan, why on earth dont you read Byron instead of reading books about him? How much would you know about me if you read what
people write about me instead of going to the original ? I can remember
reading The Corsair, The Giaour (call it The Jower) and all the rest of
them when I was a boy. I dont suppose I could read them now ; but they
had glamor for me then. Some years ago I read Don Juan through again, and
can recommend it. In fact I think you ought to read all the long poems
straight through as a culture task, except Childe Harold, which need only
be dipped into, as it is a travel book. Years later, when I was nearing
twenty,Shelley got me ; and I went into him head over heels and read every
word he published. That was a sort of literary falling in love : Shelley's
kingdom was not of this world for me. If you are really in love, this will
not make you yawn ; but I must stop, for all that.

When I tell you of my movements I am not warning you off. Little
liar : how dare you ? Honest Injun, though, you may put suspicions like
that out of your head : you overrate my delicacy and my cowardice. I will
tell you anything of that sort straight enough when I want to.

There goes the dinner bell. Adieu -- for the moment.

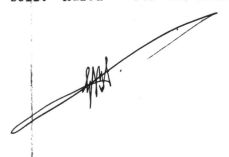

Atholl Palace. Pittochry.
Perth. Scotland.
14th July 1924

Dear Mollymollytompkins

I hope Dubs is re-established in health as well as in habitation. I have seen animals come back from such adventures with large holes in them and their scratched-out eyes hanging round their necks; but in a few days they came all right, like tuberculous-jointed children in sunbaths.

I see no reason on earth why you should not go to Italy. Everybody should go to Italy. Goethe's visit to Italy produced an extraordinary effect on him. My first visit to Italy produced Candida. But remember that the spring and the end of autumn are the best times to go. The hot season, with no rain and clouds of mosquitos, is very trying on the plains. And Carrara has no reputation as a pleasure, health, or culture resort. You must stay in Venice for at least a week, and go out to Torcello in a gondola(if there is one left); for Venice is a quite peculiar place: Then there is Verona, with a lovely church (San Zeno) and a charm of its own. Mantua is a stinking place, with pictures of extraordinary cleverness and beastliness by Giulio Romano, atoned for by the frescoes of Mantegna in the Archives. Besides, you can walk along the marshes and see the green frogs taking headers off the dock leaves as you approach. I was never in Ravenna; but I still want to go there to see the mosaics. In Milan, which is unavoidable, and about as romantic as Manchester, do not fuss about the cathedrals (a sort of fortified wedding cake) but do not miss San Ambrogio: it will give rest to your soul, which the cathedral will only worry.

M.T. maintained that she did not really want to act, that she had done so mostly to please L.T. What she wanted was to live. He therefore agreed to take her to Forte dei Marmi in Italy, where they could rent a villa by the sea. There he could get Carrara marble for his sculpture. She, to keep herself busy, took up the old craft of bookbinding and leather tooling.

Bookbinding is a first rate craft for women. I know Katherine Adams, who had a bindery in Broadway (the one in the Cotswolds, not in New York) and used to bind books for the Bodleian for 200 guineas or so. But do not pity the binders who do only one scrap of the job. They make so much more money that way that whenever an idealistic employer offers to let them change about, they refuse. I know Cobden-Sanderson, and have heard him lecture on binding. All this lettering and binding is quite good for you. Of course you will not make good on the stage unless you stick to it; but I rather doubt whether the stage is really your job: you are neither a very ignorant egotist nor a superficially lively and fundamentally brainless person, and therefore you may not find it worth your while to sacrifice everything else to acting.

Never mind W. H. H.'s demand for a crime. I should not be surprised by your writing an effective play; for your literary faculty is unmistakeable. But you must not accept other people's plots, although you may steal them. Remember that if you accept even the name of a character from another person, that other person may put in a legal claim to be your collaborator and to take half your fees. You cannot be too careful until your play comes into rehearsal; and then, strange to say, the producer may alter the whole play and even write in additional acts (if you let him), yet the copyright in all his additions and alterations belongs to you, not to him.

I am writing this in the Highlands; but as I passed last night in a sleeping car, mostly reading O'Neill's plays I am good for nothing today: hence the deadness of this letter.

G.B.S.

Oban (in Scotland). 27th August 1924

Molly, Molly, will it never cease raining? I cannot remember such another August since before I was married; and I was married before you were born.

I read your letters diligently. I even read them aloud to my wife (with an occasional skip); but I cannot answer them, for a horribly prosaic reason. I hesitate to buy a portable typewriter just as I hesitated twenty years ago (or so) to take to spectacles. But the truth, which I cannot fight off any longer, is that I am getting writer's cramp rather badly, and must either, like Barrie, learn to write with my left hand, or go in for a portable Remington. It is odd that I can still write shorthand beautifully; but I am writing this slowly and with difficulty, because my little finger _will_ drag in towards my pen and curl up my hand. You see, I was 68 on the 26th of last month.

Mrs Lawrence Tompkins
Hotel Bellevue Bristol
Pavino. Rapallo.

Italy

And that explains also why I was so shy at Godalming. I gather that another gentleman of my age, and famous for his good looks and charm, was bolder; and you see what happened to _him_! La Rochefoucauld says that the very old and the very young, if they desire to avoid making themselves ridiculous, should never allude to the garden at Godalming. However, I have still two years of youth left; so make the most of them.

Read whatever you come across or want to read. Nobody can find your proper food for you: you must find it for yourself. You ought to have read all the big things in your childhood. You may as well learn Italian now you have the chance, and read Pirandello, and tell me what he is like. I have seen his Henry IV and his Six Characters in Search of an Author: that is all. Then there is Boccaccio and a few pages of Dante.

But reading is mostly only killing time. Do not suppose that you were stagnating with Mildowed Michael because you had not time to read. I should say you were developing very rapidly. Development is a subconscious process which, I should say, stops dead the moment you begin to think about it.

The reason that there is an "I should say" in both of the last two sentences is that the first was written last Wednesday, and the second today, which is Sunday

Having stopped at Lake Maggiore and Rapallo, where they went to see Max Beerbohm and Gordon Craig, and, having run out of money, they decided to walk from Rapallo to Forte dei Marmi, well over a hundred miles along the coast.

the 31st. Between the two I made a pilgrimage to Iona by sea. But perhaps you dont know about St Columba and Fingal's cave. St Columba was an Irishman who tried to convert the Scots to Christianity, just as St Patrick was a Scot who tried to convert Ireland to the same creed. Both failed signally.

I cannot spontaneously approve of your extravagance and fecklessness in money matters. I quite see that Mrs Hilton Young (ci devant Lady Scott) and Clare Sheridan, both of them formidable rivals of yours, have done amazing things that my confounded prudence and apprehensive foresight have prevented me from doing, especially in travelling; but they both start with a handbag containing a nightdress and a broken comb, and care no more for clothes than I do. When I see a woman who buys clothes and personal paraphernalia recklessly, and goes about with a menagerie of pet animals, I write her off as impossible. No nation, and a fortiori no man can afford the friendships of such a woman. Read the history of Nelson's Lady Hamilton, Emma of the Celestial Bed.

My little finger is turning in: I can no more.

ever
G. Bernard Shaw

PS. Until Wednesday the 16th I shall be at Gleneagles Hotel, Perthshire.

Mrs. Hilton Young, an English sculptress, the former wife of Captain Scott the antarctic explorer, married to Hilton Young, later Lord Kennet.

Clare Sheridan, an American-born sculptress, author, foreign correspondent, wife of Wilfrid Sheridan, killed in World War I.

19th October 1924.

AYOT ST LAWRENCE, WELWYN, HERTS.
STATION:WHEATHAMPSTEAD,L.&N.E.R.2¼ MILES.
TELEGRAMS:BERNARD SHAW, CODICOTE.

IO, ADELPHI TERRACE. W.C.2.

Dear Madamollytompkins

In reply to your esteemed favor of the 6th instant, I am making election speeches, a degrading exhibition which you have not witnessed, and I hope never will. At every election I say This will be the last : I can stand no more of it. But when it comes to the point I see some way of handling the issues that nobody else does, and try my platform athleticism again with it. Russia has got me this time.

You ought to go to Russia : Italy is vieux jeu. Yesterday on my way down to Northampton I had with me a bundle of reports of the speeches of our great party leaders, and a half crown book by Trotsky on Problems of Life. For sheer coarse savage bloodymindedness it would be hard to beat the orations of Birkenhead, Lloyd George, and Churchill. For good sense, unaffected frankness, and educated mental capacity give me Trotsky all the time. To turn from the presidential campaign in your country and the general election here to his surveys of the position is to move to another planet.

An American quaker woman who went out to Russia to help the starving children during the famine, called on me on her way back to her family in America. I asked her was she not glad to escape from the horrors of Bolshevism to the decency of Boston (or wherever it was). She said she could not express how she grudged the three months she was going to have to spend at home. I asked her did she intend to marry a Russian or an American. She said promptly, xx a Russian if she could get one ; but they were prejudiced against foreigners. I asked her why she xxxxxx had not married Trotsky, to whom she had given lessons in English. "Oh" she said : "he is married already", plainly implying thet life in the arms of Trotsky would have been heaven on earth. She was going back to Russia in despair because she was not a Russian, finding no other country bearable after it.

Now if this is the effect Russia had on a New England quakeress, what would it have on Sarah of Red Gulch ? It seems so ridiculously old fashioned and prim to be touring Italy in the footsteps of the Victorians when this land of terror, romance, hope, and dawning is open to you with no worse discomforts than the road from Pisa to Carrara. Lawrence would get society enough there : a sculptor with a beautiful wife can go anywhere. And you need not have read Karl Marx if you can say you have read Trotsky (by my advice). your head which will amuse

Now I have put an idea into ~~~~~~~~~~~ you for a day or two. And, like the quakeress, you can come back and tell me all about it.

G. B. S.

IO ADELPHI TERRACE
LONDON W.C.2.

1st November 1924.

Bellissima Molli

I must withdraw my rash advice about Russia. Since I
wrote we have had a general election here, the result of which
will put into power in a few days a government morally at war
with the Soviet Government; and if the moral war develops into a
war of blood and iron, as it quite possibly may, an English speaking woman, however beauteous, may not be safe in Russia: the ar-
dent patriots, governed by their Kukluxes instead of by reason,
might tear her to pieces first, and listen to her explanations
that she was an American afterwards.

And if she were rash enough to make her place of origin
more precise by mentioning Georgia, they, not making fine geo-
graphical distinctions, would as likely as not conclude that she
was a Caucasian Georgian, and hurl her into the fortress of Peter
and Paul. Therefore wait a bit until we see what is going to
happen. In fact, as winter is approaching, you had better wait
until next spring; and then we can return to the subject. You
can complete your knowledge of Italian in the meantime.

I have been forgetting for a long time to relieve you
of your fear of bats. The next time a bat flies into your room,
try to persuade it to fly into a curtain and hang itself up there,
head downward, by its shoulder hooks. You must not chivy it
about, as it is quite uncatchhable in that way, and will drive any
man into red fury or any woman into hysterics. But if you can
land it in a nice thick curtain, it will not be able to resist
hanging itself up; and, it will be unable to unhook itself fast enough
to prevent you catching it. Be gentle with it, or in its terror
it may give you a mouse's bite. Take it between yourtwo palms.
You will be astonished, and will confess that you never knew what
softness meant before. A bat is the softest thing in existence.
The first touch will cure all your dislike and dread, and bring
you under its spell. Then let it out of the window, and you will
spend all the following nights, until you forget, wishing that a
bat may fly in and bring you luck.

The white oxen are very fascinating. If you buy one,
buy it at a fair or on market day. The moment you begin bargain-
ing with the owner (you would disappoint an Italian cruelly by
refusing to bargain with him) a crowd will gather. They will
join in the business enthusiastically. They will encourage you
to offer more and implore him to take less. When you pretend
that you have said your last word, and turn to go away, they will
seize you and drag you back towards the seller; and they will do
the same when he also plays that part of the game. The excitement will grow as his price and your offer approach nearer and

80

nearer, lira by lira. And when at last the difference is so
small that there is"nothing in it", the excitement will culminate
in frenzy as they seize your still half reluctant hand and force
it into his, when some elder will pronounce the benediction on
the bargain. Then you will go off with your white ox as if
nothing whatever had happened; the seller will pocket the price
with equal <u>sang froid</u>; and the crowd will disperse until a new
deal begins.

   If you doubt me, go and see next market day.

   Do you know why they think you so wonderful? They
think you are fourteen; and who could resist a fanciullina of 14
with a husband and an immense bambino - a bambinone, a bambinuc-
cio. At your age (I ask no questions) you would be an old woman
in Italy; and they dont suspect you.

   I remember one morning at Perugia standing on a hill
which had a road deeply cut through it; so that a young woman
passing through it could not see me. She had a baby - a female
baby; and she was more delighted with that baby than I have ever
seen a woman since. She sang and talked baby talk and hugged the
creature in ecstasy, calling it her Mariuccia (her great big ugly
Molly darling) in such raptures that I can still hear her. Perhaps it was you, and she was only a nursemaid; for women who like
babies at all like all babies, other people's for choice. Anyhow
that woman looked ten years older than you; and she was probably
ten years younger. So do not leave your birth certificate lying
about.

   Living in Italy is like living on Bath buns and straw-
berry ices: delicious, but you cannot keep it up. Perhaps going
to Russia with you would be the same. Anyhow I shant go: my wife
wouldn't let me.

   What has become of Bazerman's bust which was both you
and me? If he begins by being civil to you because he worships
Lawrence, he will end by being civil to Lawrence because he
worships you: a form of politeness with which Lawrence is probably fed up.

   Buona notte, bella signora: dormi bene.

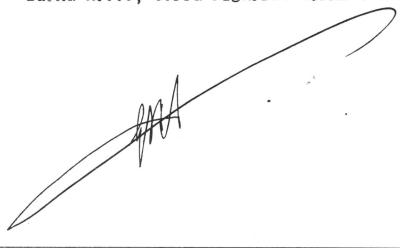

10 ADELPHI TERRACE. W.C.2.

Christmas Day 1924

Are you alive?
I sail tomorrow for
Madeira ; and my address
until the first week in February
or thereabouts will be
        Reid's Hotel
        Funchal
        Madeira .

Mrs Lawrence Tompkins
Grand Hotel
    Forte dei Marmi
        Riviera di Levante

Italy .

AYOT ST LAWRENCE, WELWYN, HERTS.,
STATION: WHEATHAMPSTEAD, G.N.R. 2¼ MILES.
TELEGRAMS: BERNARD SHAW, CODICOTE.   **22nd February 1925.**   10 ADELPHI TERRACE, W.C.2.

Mollytompkins

Dont you try to humbug me : you may do these things automatically ; but you dont do them unconsciously. You are a coquette according to the classical definition : that is, a woman who deliberately excites passions she has no intention of gratifying. If you stole that unhappy padrona's husband because you wanted him it would have been at least a reasonable proceeding ; but to steal him for the mere pleasure of stealing, and throw him away, is a wanton exercise of power, as if you broke their backs just to prove that you could do it. I dont suppose she will shoot you ; but if she does, no Latin jury will convict her, any more than they would convict Lawrence if he gave you the thrashing you deserve.

I suppose it is no use telling you to be careful. Coquettes and Philanderers are incorrigible. I remember a well known poetess (now no more) saying to me, when I refused to let her commit adultery with me, "You had no right to write the preface if you were not going to write the book". In those remote days I had not yet realized that the old fashioned Irish convention of gallantry, by which every gentleman was expected to pretend that his heart was at the feet of any lady he happened to be talking to, was not current in England, and that an Englishwoman might take as a serious proposal what an Irishwoman would laugh away as a polite flattery. But the phrase is worth remembering. You go about the world writing prefaces without the least intention of writing the books ; and the sooner you realize that what is fun to you is heartbreak and homebreak to your victims, the better. Not that that will stop you ; for the instinct which delights in dancing on the edge of a precipice when you have lured a giddy man there, knowing that your own head is sound and that you can get back in safety, is incurable. But no woman who knows the mischief she is doing is quite so reckless as one who doesnt.

Remember also that homicide is much commoner in Italy than in England, and much more privileged when it is a reaction of sexual infatuation. So when you go husband stealing dont forget your gun.

~~XXXXXXXXXXXXXXXXXXXXXXXXXXXXXXXXXXXXXXXXXXX~~

I have been in Madeira for six weeks. Your last letter broke off with a sick bed on which you were apparently dying ; and I began to wonder whether you were alive. Your letter about Achilles is at least reassuring on that point. You are, if anything, far too much alive.

24th February 1925.

But now comes another letter which makes me doubt whether I should send you what I have already written. I ask the heavens despairingly is the human race becoming incapable of living without surgical operations. Only the other day a friend of mine wrote from Italy that he was going on the table -- it was in Florence too ; but they tell me the operation has been a great sucess. In Madeira I met a woman who had been ill for fifteen years ; and she, also, had been operated on and cured so completely that she learnt to dance the tango with me (I learnt it myself because it appeared to me to be the only dance left that really is a dance, and when I had worked myself after breakfast into congestion of the brain, and smoothed myself out again by plunging into the gulf stream at 64 F. before lunch, there was nothing else to do after sitting in the sun until I was bored but pay the professional expert to teach me the modern dances, as I dont play tennis and am no more tempted by roulette than a croupier is). I utterly disbelieve in the modern school of operative surgery; but its practice is often more successful than its reasoning ; and I have met several people who declared they were the better for it and were sorry they had not got it done sooner. So I am not at all convinced that I shall never see you again.

I will not come to Italy to share the fate of Achilles. Besides, I am not nearly as bad as you ; and if I were to drive all the women mad and you all the men we should deported as undesirables. You see, at Prior's Field I was bound to behave very well indeed for the credit of the Society ; and I had not only use screens of conversation, but actually to hold you between me and ladies who wouldnt behave themselves.

The Russian letter would not interest you : it had exactly the effect I meant it to have. I must educate these idiots.

Morris made all sorts of chairs : there is no particular Morris chair that I know of.

The Ghibellines were the party of the Emperor -- of the Holy Roman Empire — who aspired to be in politics what the Pope was in religion. The Guelphs were the men of the free cities, who werent having any Holy Roman Empire.

Unless I close this and send it now it will never go. Heaven send it may find you well again.

G.B.S.

Prior's Field was a Fabian Summer School in Surrey where, before going on a long motor tour of England with them, Shaw had invited L.T. and M.T. to help screen him from the advances of an overzealous redheaded Fabian.

84

10, ADELPHI TERRACE. W.C.2.

1st June 1925

AYOT ST. LAWRENCE, WELWYN, HERTS.
STATION: WHEATHAMPSTEAD, G.N.R. 2¼ MILES.
TELEGRAMS: BERNARD SHAW, CODICOTE.

I am laid low by influenza, which struck me down on the platform at Kings College immediately after I had made a delightful speech without the faintest premonition of the catastrophe. I rallied, relapsed, rallied again, relapsed again, and am now crawling precariously back to my normal condition.

I have not finished my book on Socialism; and all the stories about my writing another play are canards.

I am tickled by Achilles behaving exactly as the men do in my comedies when the women take the initiative. You had better write a book about him unless you are really learning the painter's trade.

You must really get a profession. Playtime will not last forever. And Lawrence may bolt any day with some irresistible signorina who will spend every rap he possesses.

G.B.S.

10 ADELPHI TERRACE. W.C.2.

25th June 1925.

Next time you happen to be writing, tell me what you know about one Mollie Little, who alleges that she kept house for you, and on that score asks me with extraordinary persistence for sums of money in three figures, undaunted by the dead silence into which her letters fall. I hesitated to give her away to you when the letters poured in at first; and I should strongly deprecate your remonstrating with her, as any recognition of her existence would be fatal; but as I am pretty certainly not the only friend of yours she is trying, you had better know.

Laurence will certainly be vamped, and elope. You have trained him to be imposed on.

G. B. S.

Miss Mollie Little was drama critic on the Plymouth newspaper who reviewed M.T.'s performances. When her family went broke, M.T. hired her as a secretary to run her house in London while she was acting or on the road.

86

Telegrams—"Pentland Hotel. Thurso."
Phone—Thurso 10.

Loch Fishing Free to Residents.
Garage with Private Lock-ups.

PENTLAND HOTEL, THURSO.

MISSES HARPER, Proprietors. 9th August 1925

Cara Mollia

Miss Little is no trouble : her letters rather amused me ; and her cheerful perseverance would have made me good-humored enough to give her a tip if I had not known that I might just as well have adopted her until death did us part. You have never given me the slightest unwelcome trouble .

We are touring about (so that the servants may have holidays and the painters and repairers do their worst) in the extreme north of Scotland, where, thanks to the Gulf Stream, the climate is most unexpectedly like the extreme south of any other country. Tomorrow we cross to "the islands" (Orkneys & Shetlands) and are re-reading Scotts Pirate accordingly. He writes as I wrote at 23 as far as the dialogue of genteel persons is concerned ; but as a story teller and entertainer he beats hollow all the fearfully clever modern women whose books make one miserable. It is a case of Shakespear and Scott first and the rest (save one) nowhere .

We are not, by the way, in the old car, but in its contemptuous and impetuous successor, a Vauxhall . When you are tired of Italy, try the Shetlands for a change. I like the Scots (though the Shetlanders, by the way, are Norse) because they combine the noblest sentiments and the loftiest imagination with an utter inability to resist the slightest temptation, whether of the world, the flesh, or the devil. Like the Italians, by the way.

This is a wet Sunday; and for want of a fixed address no letters have reached me since Thursday. Hence leisure to write to thee, or, in purest Tuscan, a te O cara. But keep your heart still: "a te O cara" is only the name of a quartet from Bellini's Puritani, in which my mother sang when I was a child — not, however, that that really spoils it.

Dont worry about Sir J. and Miss L. He is a Scot, and must have an enormous experience of borrowers. I have just written him a long letter about his book, which I read when I was ill. I was ill for exactly 30 days, collapsing with a crash and recovering in a flash: two miracles. I am now as well as I ever shall be.

I had to pay 2½ excess postage on your letter. I bore it bravely because it meant that the letter was a long one; but I mention it because you may have less devoted correspondents. For some reason all Americans believe that a 2 cent stamp will carry any letter anywhere.

How did the holiday from Laurence (or for Laurence) turn out? He will die of you unless he spends 8 hours a day in a studio, or, as the Americans say, an office, which you never approach. I hope Ettore (or is it Sheelay?) will fall in love with someone else — his wife, for instance —

AYOT ST LAWRENCE, WELWYN, HERTS.
STATION: WHEATHAMPSTEAD, G.N.R. 2¼ MILES.   15th December 1925.   IO ADELPHI TERRACE. W.C.2.
TELEGRAMS: BERNARD SHAW, CODICOTE.

My dear Molly

Do not be deterred from writing whenever you feel inclined by my apparent irresponsiveness. I must get my book on Socialism out. I find that if I answer letters it stops ; and if I let everything else go smash -- even your feelings -- it goes on. I sit in a calm centre, with a typhoon of the fury of the unanswered raging all round.

I really cannot stand your not going to the Théatre des Arts and telling me whether la Pitoeff (to whom I have just posted a most lovilly portrait of myself in a copy of the Ricketts édition de luxe of St Joan)is really so exquisite all over as she seems to be from her pictures, and from the ravings of all who have seen her in the part. You say you cannot leave Lawrence. That is nonsense : the vampire can always take a few hours off, especially if her prey is so exhausted that he cannot move until she comes back. Go at once, I order you.

You know you should not have taken that wretched dog to Paris. Its doom was certain. However, your letters would not be so amusing if you had a scrap of prudence or foresight. I never do anything because I am prudent and foresee everything. My life lacks the imprevu.

But you might at least have foreseen that in Paris, glutted with Americanesses, all determined to be the dernier cri, and with arty students worshipping Shaws of one sort or another, your stocks could not stand so high as they did in the much healthier atmosphere of Liguria. The Parisians are not French, and have the worst manners of any people in the world. Frenchwomen, even outside Paris, mistake a depressing and parsimonious neatness for taste in dress (of which they are utterly void), and go into mourning for their twentieth cousins as an excuse for always wearing black : the only resource of people who cannot dress because they have no color sense. Try Toulouse if you want to meet violently French people. Take the car (when the spring comes) and try the country between the Rhone (Valence) and Toulouse. It is lovely. But when the season is advanced enough to make it faibly sure that the snow is off the passes make for the Savoy and Dauphiné. Go to Annecy and stay in the Beau Rivage Hotel. Read as much of Rousseau's Confessions as you can stand ; and spend every day going over one mountain pass and coming back over another.

M.T. did go to see Ludmilla Pitoeff play *Saint Joan* in the Paris production and found her disappointing. Subsequently when she played the part at the Globe in London in 1930 Shaw was equally disappointed.

Go over into Italy and back. Over the Galibier zigzag up to the tunnel at the top of the world, and wander about amid a sea of peaks to give the car time to cool down (it will probably be boiling like mad). Go on from Annecy to Grenoble, and put in another fortnight there doing the same thing. There is nothing in the way of motoring in France, or indeed anywhere else, to be compared to it. But you must join the Touring Club de France and get a triptyque for Italy and Switzerland as well as France ; for you will be in and out of these countries, or the Nomansland between them, almost every day ; and the douane is inexorable.

In the south you can go right along the tops of the Pyrenees-from .. Bayonne to Perpignan on the edge of Spain without ever going across the frontier (no harm in having Spain on your triptyque though) and back again on the low ground, seeing Gavarni and Lourdes and a lot of pretty places in the Pyrenean Basque valleys. At Lourdes you can give Lawrence a drink from the miraculous well, and cure him.

It will teach you mountain driving, which is enormously better fun than blinding along the endless straight military roads on the flat.

Charlotte has just bought Cabel's Figures of Earth : I must look through it when we arrive at the Falmouth Hotel, Falmouth, Cornwall, next Monday for a Christmas away-from-home of three weeks or thereabouts. We shall pass by Stonehenge. Do you remember ?
Charlotte greatly admires your other pet book. I, alas ! began it, and was quite pleased with it until, about thirty pages from the beginning, I suddenly realized that there was nothing on earth to prevent his going on like that for ever. Like Francesca and her lover, in that book I read no more.

What about that golf ball ? It is useless to pretend that I have any illusions about doctors ; and it is useless to say anyting until I have the latest news ; but I naturally want to know. By the way, was that Florentine operation a success ? it is long enough ago now for you to know ; and it is as much my business as anyone else's.

You wrote me a gorgeous letter from Civita Vecchia after Rome. Did I express my appreciation ? I never could make out what happened to the furniture of that villa. As far as I could gather you left it in the hotel at Viareggio when you fled by the 2-55 train.

My three months in Scotland motoring in the mountains was a great success from the health point of view. I think I am better than I was last year though I have no time to bother about it. We went right up to Shetland. Anyhow, I got through my Fabian lecture in fine form. I enjoy struggling with The Intelligent Woman's Guide to Socialism and

The note reads:

Anyhow, I got through my Fabian lecture in fine form. I enjoy struggling with The Intelligent Woman's Guide to Socialism and Capitalism because it is real brain work, not romancing and inventing, but reasoning hard. It brushes me up and renews my hardy youth. After all, I shan't be 70 until next July. There is some work left in me yet. And I have actually written you quite a long letter. Let me hear from you, but not until you have seen St. Joan. You can lock Lawrence up in the cellar until you come back. Or even take him with you. He can't be more troublesome than poor Yak, whom I am assuming to have been strychnined.
                    Your quite affectionate
                                    G.B.S.

Charlotte is G.B.S.'s wife, born Charlotte Frances Payne-Townsend, in Ireland in 1857, whom Shaw married at the turn of the century.

Ayot St Lawrence, Welwyn, Herts.
27th January 1926.

Dearest Molly

Yes : I am distracted by the slowness with which the book is proceeding through the press. However, it does me good to have to do a real hard literary job, all brains, instead of writntgplays. Writing letters is impossible : this is only to explain why I cannot write them.

I snatch this moment late in the evening, when I should not write at all. I am alone here, my wife having gone up to town. It is the anniversary of Mozart's birth in 1756 (I followed in 1856); and his Little Night Music is coming through on the wireless. It is a mild night ; and I am sitting at the fire with my typewriter on my knees, like a sailor with his lass.

When Lady Lavery went to New York lately our parting so affected her that -- more enterprising than you -- she kissed me in broad daylight before all the world in Cromwell Place. But it was spoilt by our meeting again next day at lunch at Mary Borden's. When the party broke up Lady Lavery said "I kissed him yesterday in the middle of the street". "Kiss him again by all means" said Mary. "I can't" said Lady Lavery : "he struggles so".

All three ladies are American. The third is you. But you, being the youngest, do not understand that dotards of seventy must not assume that beautiful females who admire their works would like to be pawed by them. There is a shyness of (youth) as there is a shyness of (age). And that is only the cheapest out of a dozen reasons why a man, especially an old man, does not always devour his natural prey.

Transpose

Mary Borden is an American author; Lady Lavery, the wife of Sir John Lavery, the English portrait painter.

And then, your romance has lasted a long time without spoiling. There are moments, of course, when you want to consummate it. But they pass ; and the romance remains. You get tired of waiting ; but suppose there were no longer anything to wait for !

But these things do not fit into words and arguments. They belong to the Elysian fields (not those through which you rush the Renault, but those that Gluck set to music in Orfeo) into which we both want to escape to meet each other, and in which we never shall meet ~~except~~ except in imagination. But we shall do as well on this solid earth as we need ; for next time you will not be so tongue tied to say the least.

You not say how Lawrence is. After Lawrence has to be con. Do not have another operati er. When you have a pain, and money, the doctors say they will open you up, and cut the pain out. They open you up accordingly, and cut out anything that they think you will not miss ; but the pain comes back all the same until it cures itself.

Tolstoy's daughter told me terrible things about the Bolsheviks the other day ; but when I asked her whether she would exchange the Moscow Government for the French or English or American one, she started (like Juliet) and said No.

Write when you please and how you please. Your letters are extremely readable (my wife is quite keen on them) and they make me feel romantic at times, which is pleasant at my age. After all, I shall not be completely seventy until July.

Are you really going back to Forte ? As a rule, it is a mistake to go back anywhere. When you read my book to Lawrence and Baby it is they and not you who will go asleep. By the way, stop calling him Baby : the other children will laugh at him; and boys are frightfully sensitive. I remember how I hated being called Sonny. You yourself want to be called Marie instead of Molly ; but I think Mary should be reserved for the Blessed Virgin, or rather the Blessed Mother.

As you are in Paris, why not take lessons in declamation? We are no good at that in Gower St.

The note reads:

You yourself want to be called Marie instead of Molly; but I think Mary should be reserved for the Blessed Virgin, or rather the Blessed Mother.
As you are in Paris, why not take lessons in Declamation? We are no good at that in Gower St.

       GBS

Dictated.

STATION: WHEATHAMPSTEAD, L.& N.E.R. 2¼ MILES.
TELEGRAMS: BERNARD SHAW, CODICOTE.

My dear Soave Maria

Your letter has been read to me, & has helped to bring down my temperature to normal. By the time this reaches you I shall be up & about but letter writing is out of the question. Letter reading, however, is most beneficial & agreeable.

Sempre a te

G.B.S.

10, ADELPHI TERRACE. W.C.

12th July 1926.

AYOT ST LAWRENCE, WELWYN, HERTS.
STATION: WHEATHAMPSTEAD, G.N.R. 2¼ MILES.
TELEGRAMS: BERNARD SHAW, CODICOTE.

At last an address!

You mean the Borromean island in Lago Maggiore, dont you? I must go and have a look at it if I survive my 70th birthday the Monday after next.

You must settle down somewhere. You have been living the life of a lost dog, and making Lawrence live it instead of sticking in a stoneyard as a sculptor should.

A heat wave has suddenly smitten us here after a long coldish spring. I am forced to go on working instead of taking a leaf out of your book (which is what I need); but for this last day or so I have been feeling a little as if I were going to live a while longer.

G.B.S.

The note at the top of the page was dictated by Shaw to his wife, C.F.S.

019274 FOT. D. MENAPACE - STRESA N. 854

Is it this one ? All the others
look too big for the price.

Mrs Laurence Tompkins
Bankers Trust Company
5 Place Vendôme
Paris
France.

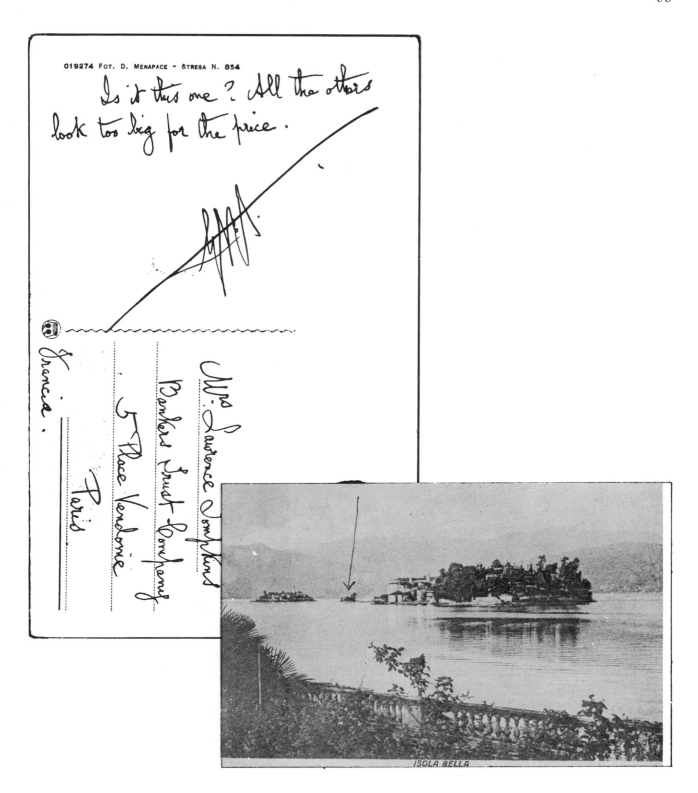

ISOLA BELLA

053474 FOT. D. MENAPACE - STRESA

I thought at first it might be this — the Madre. But the house looks too large for three; and they tell me it has been sold to a millionaire Torinese. But after all you behave like a millionaire. Still, Henry remonstrates.

Francia.

Banker
5 Pla

M. Laure

STRESA

Lago Maggiore - CARCIANO e ISOLE BORROMEE

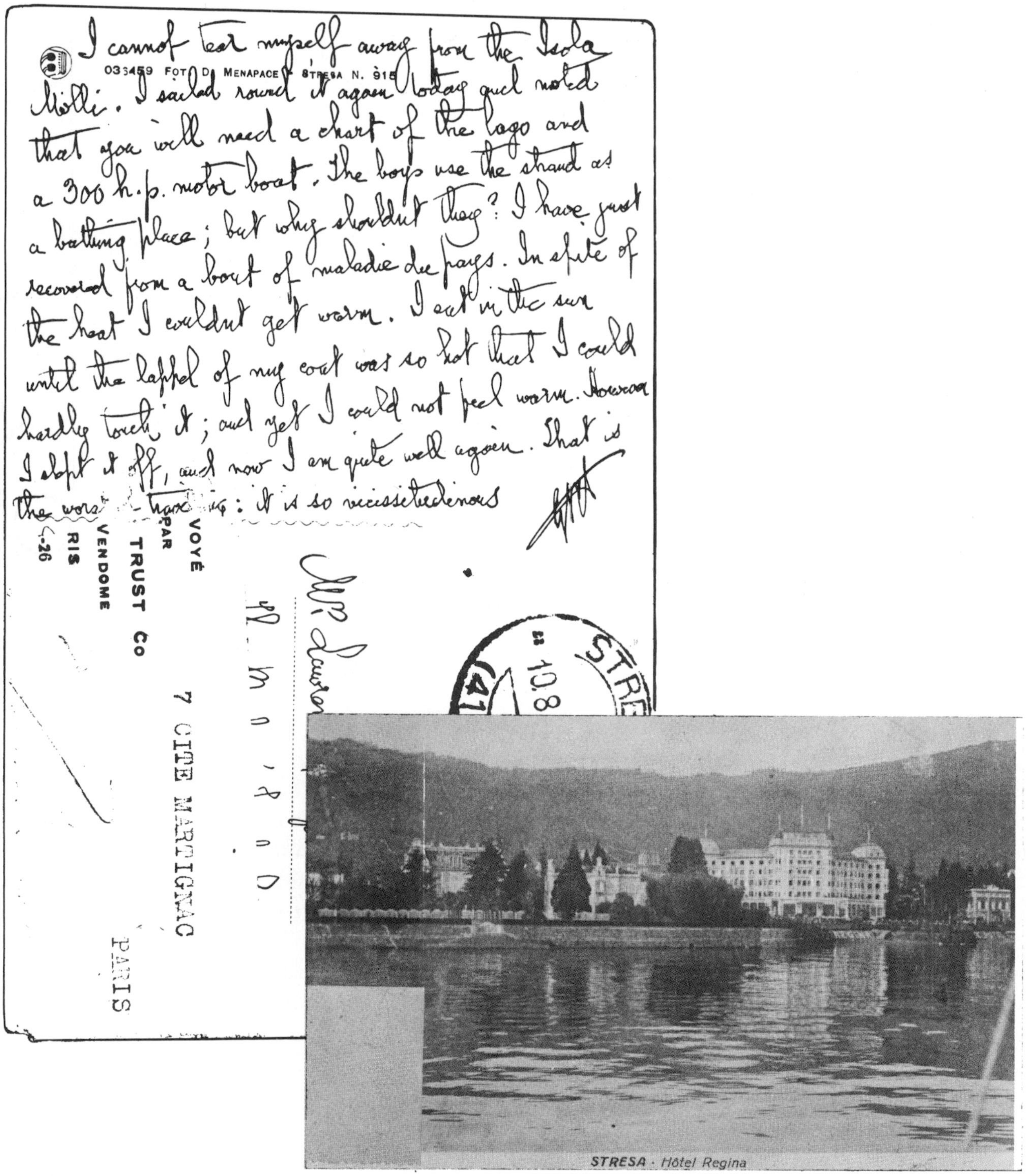
I cannot tear myself away from the Isola Mölli. I sailed round it again today and noted that you will need a chart of the lago and a 300 h.p. motor boat. The boys use the strand as a bathing place; but why shouldnt they? I have just recovered from a bout of maladie du pays. In spite of the heat I couldnt get warm. I sat in the sun until the lappel of my coat was so hot that I could hardly touch it; and yet I could not feel warm. However I slept it off, and now I am quite well again. That is the worst of travelling: it is so vicissitudinous

The last sentence reads:

That is the worst of travelling: it is so vicissitudinous

8th August 1926
Regina Palace Hotel
B. Bossi, Proprietaire-Directeur

Stresa (Lac Majeur)
(Ligne du Simplon) Loetschberg

Molly, Mollissima

Only think! I sailed round those islands yesterday. I should be very poetic about it had you not unfortunately told me you were taking one of them. The poet became a house agent instantly. The Grand Hotel, Pallanza, with its jazzings, is right on top of you. Have you found out all about the drainage of Pallanza, to say nothing of the drainage of S. Giovanni. Certainly the water of the lake is as limpid as could be desired: I had a long swim in it. Still, make sure.

Today, after much lightning last night, there came a combination of burning sun and agitating wind that laid me low. I am a little better, but can hardly write. And a most appalling thing happened at noon. The hotel porter dashed in and announced the Princess Borromeo, the governor of the provinzia of Novara, half a dozen mayors and ex-mayors, and countless marchesane, principesse, contesse, baronesse d'ogni grado nobile. Charlotte and I stood aghast; but there was no time to fly. The princess fortunately talked English, and unbent before my blarney. With perfect tact she took her crowd away after a short visit; but they all invited us to call.

She knew there was a lady who was taking S. Giovanni, but did not know her name. I said you were a friend.

I doubt if you will stay long here. You should never have a luxury as part of your daily fare: you cannot live on Neapolitan ices; and if you try you will loathe them. You should live and work in a commonplace way, and keep the luxuries for holidays.

Lawrence is right: the day for deserting America to live in Europe as an artistic vagabond (like the sculptor Storey, whom Charlotte knew quite well) is gone by; and in spite of the Babbits and Fundamentalists America, now completely cock of the walk, is beginning at last to produce an art of her own. You ought not to keep him in Europe. But three months on the island every year will be enough for you.

I agree about the Leviathan. The old cheap ten-day ships must be far the best. A ship is a ship; and a hotel is a hotel: what God hath disjoined let no man put together.

Your letter came this morning.

I can no more. I left London stupid with fatigue; and though crossing the Alps bucked me, as it always does, for a two days rally, I have relapsed today to zero, and can send you only this most perfunctory reply.

ever
G.B.S.

L.T. and M.T. rented the Borromeo island off Pallanza called Isolino San Giovanni, which they made their permanent home till the Wall Street crash of 1929 obliged them to leave it in 1931.

The reverse of this postcard from Charlotte Shaw reads:

Hotel Regina. 22 Aug 1926

Thank you, dear, for your nice letter. I am sorry you suffered on the journey, but how good you had some one to look after you.

G.B.S. gets better & better. I think I shall have to bring him to live here!

This dirty postcard is the only one in Stresa of San Giovanni, but they have promised to get some more.

I will do what you ask about books to the best of my ability: but it cannot be until I go back to England. Our love to you both.   C.F.S.

Strosa. 3ᵈ Sptᵇ 1926.

I received your letter, with contents as stated, after a discussion which ended in my going back to the hotel for my passport. Many thanks; but in future dont register. I never do unless I want to have legal proof of having sent the letter.

Lewis had to rush back to London yesterday on intelligence that his house has been burgled, and Dushinka's fur coat stolen. Simultaneously I was discovered by Prince Paul Troubetskoy the sculptor, who has a villa at Suna, a suburb of Pallanza. His old bust of me looks very much alive. He insists on making a miniature full length of me: I sit (or stand) for the first time tomorrow. I have been too ill to write before; but a culminating headache yesterday has left me almost well. G.B.S.

Lago Maggiore.   Baveno ed Isola Superiore.

99

Stresa. 3rd Sep 1926

Yes, yes: I got your bothersomely honest letter. I sent you a card this morning to say so. If you have started being afraid of me, all is over. Lots of people are: that is why they hate me. The fear of God may be the beginning of wisdom; but the fear of Man is the beginning of murder.

Ask Lawrence what he thinks of the other side of this card for sculpture. The two figures are terra cotta statues. At Varallo, two hours from here by car, the Sacro Monte has 42 chapels with scenes like this one. I have made the pilgrimage twice. Read Samuel Butler's Alps & Sanctuaries, and fancy that it is written by me. And don't spell my politics politics.

Mrs Law
1 Rue
Paris VII
France

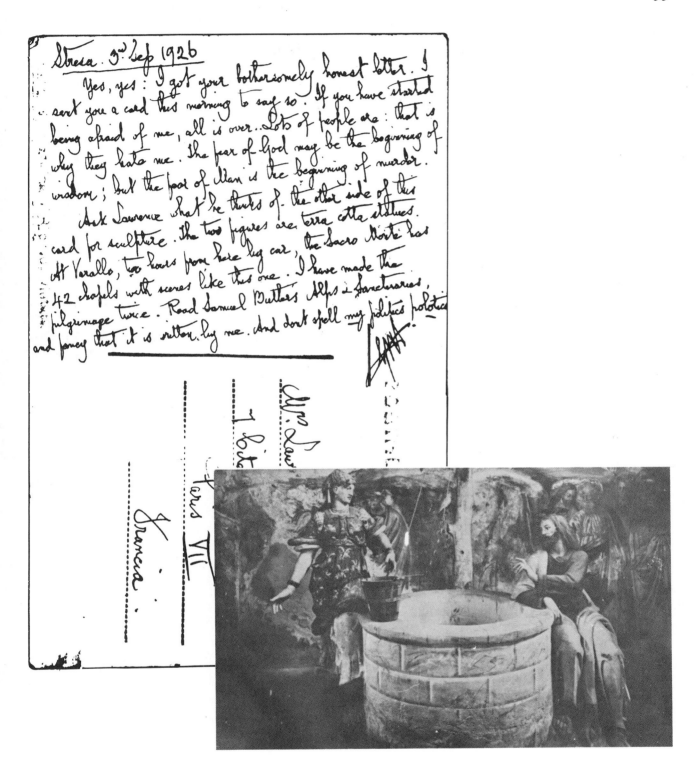

Regina Palace Hotel
B. Bossi, Proprietaire-Directeur

10 Sep. 1926   Stresa (Lac Majeur)

Dear Molly

Thank you in sending me such a nice letter. Of course it is "all right" for you to write to me, your letters are delightful, only, my dear, you must not expect me to answer. My life is so busy & rushed & occupied that if I allowed myself the luxury of keeping up correspondences I should never have one moment to get quiet, or restful or meditative & I should become a terribly nervy, tiring person! And, not to speak of the time they take up; writing letters itself is rather nervy, distracting work don't you think.

We are going on in just the same way we were when you left. The Lewises went back to London—he in a great fuss, she quite calm,—at a day's notice because their house had been broken into there & a lot of things stolen. It is hard upon them, poor dears, they care so much for "things"—at least *he* does—but most of the things stolen were hers—fur coats & embroideries . . .

We have made real friends with the Coates. I have got to like them both very much. He is a real genius, splendid & capable—she is devoted & fine & has given up her own career to help to make his. I don't mean I admire *that*: only I can't help admiring *her!* Then there has turned up Prince Paul Troubetskoi. He has a villa & studio near Pallanza & is a very considerable sculptor. Perhaps Lawrence will know about him. He did a bust of G.B.S. in London in 1912—we hated it then, but it is here now in his studio & we are amazed to find how much we like it. He is doing a small statuette now,—G.B.S. sitting, leaning right back, a tiny thing. After that he wants to do a head. It keeps G.B.S. amused & interested talking art to him & music to Mr. Coates, so that is good.

In one thing you amazed me in your letter. You say you will ask Bumpus about books on religion to read to Peter. Molly! Molly! how young you are. Religion is of all subjects in the world the most elusive, the most dangerous, the most important, the most far-reaching, the most all-embracing: to talk or read about it to a child is the most responsible & the most anxious thing a grown-up could possibly have to do. I shrank from the idea of advising until I got back & could be with my own books & ask a dear old friend who lives with books & religion what he thought about it: & now—you say—you'll ask a book seller! . . !

We have made no plans about going back yet. I expect we'll stay here until the end of the month. It has done G.B.S. good, & he is amused & rather happy here: but alas! he is not *well*. not as he was before last March.

The Island looks very sweet. I often look up to the place where we had that most wonderful dinner!

By the way Prince Paul looks forward to visiting you. He says he knew the Island well in the time of the Duchess of Sermoneta. It seems he did the two monuments on the piazza at Pallanza. We have studied them with him. The little war memorial is very beautiful.

Ever,

C.F.S.

Cecil Lewis, an English writer, and his Russian wife, "Dooshka," lived across the lake from the Isolino next door to the conductor Albert Coates and his wife, Madelon.

I

CARTOLINA POSTALE

CARTE POSTALE

Regina Palace Hotel, Stresa, 14th Sept. 1926.

My dear Molly

Your life seems to be one of considerable quite unnecessary friction. But I will not preach.

I must, however, be allowed to say that "tackless", which in Red Gulch means absence of tack, is in England tactless, or absence of tact. And that was only one of four.

I apologize for my crossness. But if you had

CARTOLINA POSTALE

CARTE POSTALE

"RAJAR"

spent the money on something to please yourself instead of bothering me with it, I should not have turned a hair..

They still advertise the isolino as to let in the hall of this hotel. I hope you have an agreement signed. If not, and a higher bidder comes along, you may find yourself betrayed, an unbearable thought. This reminds me that English trees are bare in winter, not bear as in Red Gulch.

III

CARTOLINA POSTALE
CARTE POSTALE
"RAJAR"

Troubetskoy keeps me sitting — or (worse) standing — all the time. He has done a small seated figure, and a lifesize head which promises to be a masterpiece, though Charlotte objects that it is tragic and pessimistic. Now if the isolino had been ready, and Lawrence here ——— !!!

Poor Mrs Cecil Lewis returned to London to find her house burgled by a criminal of taste, who selected her furs, her

IV

CARTOLINA POSTALE

CARTE POSTALE

RAJAR

Chinese embroideries, her Ming china, and everything that was precious and exquisite.

Albert Coates has gone to London for 10 days to gramophone the Ninth Symphony, and left me to swim with Miss Rosenheim or Tunbetskoy.

And that, dearest Molly, I think, is all the news.

G. Bernard Shaw.

Regina Palace Hotel, Stresa, 18th Sept. 1926

This time I really am cross. What do you mean
by it, you young devil? You send a telegram to say
you are coming to see us. Then another to say you
will be at Pallanza on Saturday: no when or where.
On Saturday Charlotte gives up our bathe at Cairo and
stays in until half past two, waiting for you, or for
at least a telephone message. We conclude that your
"Saturday" meant Saturday night, and go off on our
previously arranged excursion to Orta; but, to make
sure, I leave a note telling your our movements for
tomorrow, and giving you carte blanche to join in just
as might suit you. We were both disappointed that
you had not turned up in time to come to Orta; but
I was looking forward to taking you to Trabetskoys

tomorrow to see the bust and the statuette.

On our return we find a sniffy little card "Sorry to have missed you this trip. Am returning immediately to Paris." Charlotte was much disconcerted, and distressed lest you had gone off in a huff.

"Am returning immediately to Paris."!!! . . . Return immediately to hell, you little beast, and never dare write to me or approach me or mention your poisonous island to me again as long as you live.

19th Septr. 1926.

RÉGINA PALACE HÔTEL
B. BOSSI, PROPRIETAIRE·DIRECTEUR

STRESA (LAC MAJEUR)
(LIGNE DU SIMPLON) LOETSCHBERG

My dear Molly

You are behaving like an idiot. Troubetskoy gave me your letter this afternoon, too late to do anything but leave this for you at Baveno.

We have to go on a whole day's excursion tomorrow (Monday) with the Coates.

That will give you time to pull yourself together, and come to see us sensibly on Tuesday, when I shall go over to Laveno to bathe as usual, leaving here at 10·30, and returning to lunch. In the afternoon I give Troubetskoy a final sitting.

You must behave exactly as you did before, when you were very nice. But you will spoil everything if you tomfool as you are doing now. So be good, and look in on Tuesday, clothed & in your right mind.

GBS.

'Phone: 246 **HYDRO-HOTEL**, DADDY HOLE PLAIN. **TORQUAY**. Devon 'Grams: *Hydrotel*
2207. 3755 We shall be here for another fortnight, probably.

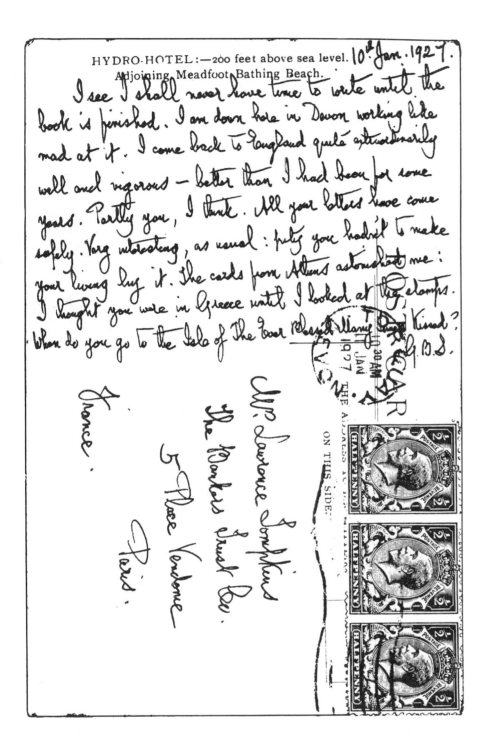

The last line of this postcard reads:

When do you go to the Isle of The Ever Blessed Many Times Kissed?

The book is *The Intelligent Woman's Guide to Socialism.*

110

12th January 1927

HYDRO HOTEL, DADDY HOLE PLAIN. TORQUAY

TELEGRAMS :
"HYDROTEL, TORQUAY."

TELEPHONE, TWO LINES:
MANAGEMENT 2207
VISITORS - 3755

ADJOINING MEADFOOT BATHING BEACH

I think you must have something more than a postcard, O Mollimia, to greet you after your journey. That
was a ghastly description of Athens, Ga. You should have
made Aunt Mary come to you instead of going to her. The
worst of an experience like that is that it comes back
years after in dreams when one is out of sorts. Ex-priso-
ners dream themselves back in prison ; ex-clerks who hated
business (like me) dream themselves back in the office ;
and you should not give Athens, Ga. TWO chances of getting back at you. Fortunately these reminiscences wear
out in the course of time. And, anyhow, you will have
the Baveno road at night, and the Cerro passage at noon,
and even the shelter at Ayot to steal into your sleep
from the past. It will take twenty years to reach that
point. Then you will wake up puzzled but pleased, and
say "That was a happy dream, somehow ; but what on earth
was the name of that old man ?"

When you say you will never go back to America I
have to remind myself that I shall soon be either dead or
such an intolerable old bore and dotard that you may have
to go back to put the seas between us. For if you did not
exist, and Lawrence asked me for any advice in that matter
I should say "America is coming to life at last. The day
for the American sculptor to live in Rome, like Storey, or to hang about the Quartier Latin, or listen reve-
rently to Frank Harris at Nice, is past and gone. Henry
James felt buried in America; but he came here only to be
enbalmed. The uprooted American withers : things are beginning to grow in the Golden West. Go back ; or at least
keep in touch. By the way, you might leave Molly behind
if you are tired of her".

This painting business is all very well ; but you
can't paint half as well as Bertha Newcombe, whose portrait of me openmouthed on the platform is still the best

painting.

vision of me at that period ; and Bertha did not go on
~~exercise~~. Unless your life depended on it you could never
practise yourself into mastery either at the easel or on
the stage; but at writing, where the elementary part of the
technique is learnt in the nursery and necessarily practised every day, your talent would not be hampered in this
way. Of course you want to paint : so did I ; but remember the lines of Cashel Byron   world,
     For know, rash youth, that in this starcrossed /
     Fate drives us all to seek our chiefest good
     In what we can, and not in what we would.
    But this is against all my vows and principles. I am
discouraging you, Heaven forgive me! Find your own way :
never mind me.
    And goodnight.

                         G.B.S.

By the way, as to our movements, we shall be here until about
the 23rd, when we shall start for Ayot. The journey takes us two days.
I must be in London on the 27th to fulfil engagements.

The Regina patriarch writes to Charlotte that the hotel is closed
for the winter, but that he hopes &c &c &c.

Christmas of 1926 M.T. and L.T. took P.T.
out of school in Paris and returned to America for a brief visit before settling on the
Isolino.

2nd February 1927

AYOT ST LAWRENCE, WELWYN, HERTS.
STATION: WHEATHAMPSTEAD, G.N.R. 2¼ MILES.
TELEGRAMS: BERNARD SHAW, CODICOTE.

10 ADELPHI TERRACE. W.C.2.

That, Mollimia, very nearly sent us spinning across the channel to come down the sun into the Lombard plain. However, we mustn't, yet. Even with Yak at large the attraction of the island is very strong.

I will say no more about the coming to life of America. If you treat it as I treated Ireland how can I object? Europe has caught you and will never let you go. But Peter! Is he to be an American, an Italian, or an English public school boy?

If Lawrence cannot get commissions in the face of Troubetskoy's competition he must keep his hand in by peopling the isle with statues. He must shew the Isola Bella people how it should really be done.

If you meet Basile, tell him that I have got into hot water with the Liberals for defending Mussolini, who, by the way, has told the world how he imposes absolute SILENCE on all his supporters. The reign of the phrasemonger, he says, is ended for ever in Italy. I thought of Basile, the best talker I know, and smiled. Here the Strong Silent Man is vieux jeu.

You reproach me for not shewing your painting to Charlotte. Bless you, dearest, that isnt painting. I liked it because it was alive enough to express the joy it gave you to splosh it down; but one doesn't shew such things about to people who have seen Turner's water colors and Monet's oils, or — in north Italy — Segantinis. You paint now as I sing and play (when nobody but Charlotte is listening), and as no doubt you dance, for the fun of it, or ride, or ski, or skate; but you couldnt make your living by it. You dont know what professional work is. You may shew your screevings to me as a child shews its drawings to a fond father; but however fond I may be I am not patherly

What nearly sent the Shaws "spinning across the channel" was a letter from M. T. describing the island in winter with snow still on the branches of the blooming camelia trees, the lake deserted, Yak, her huge dog, running wild.

enough to shew them about. My infatuation would be suspected at once. I am incorruptible in matters of art. On any other subject I can lie to please you; but in this you come up against something utterly merciless. You will have to drudge for a long time at pictures that will get worse and worse as you try to finish them before you can really capture that effect you shewed me in a competently drawn sketch in two hours. No sky looks like the thumb marks of a glazier's apprentice, however brilliantly you may color the putty. By all means go on until you find either that you can do it or can't well enough to produce something that has an existence and interest completely independent of your own — something that used you to get born as you used a brush and a tin of dirty water or turpentine — but if you are not as ashamed of your practice attempts as I was of my wretched novels your case is hopeless. The discovery that you actually wanted me to shew that daub to Charlotte has perfectly stupended me. You ought to have been ready to kill me if I had suggested it; though I might have done it behind your back to find whether she saw any promise in it.

I am not making myself agreeable; but you would get wearied if I were always nice and considerate of your feelings. Besides, you know its true. And anyhow, you must take me as I come. Accomplished and inveterate actor as I am beginning to let the mask slip occasionally and damn the consequences.

In other words I am beginning to write tired nonsense and had better go to bed and think about sacks of sawdust until I fall asleep.

Carlo Basile, a titled Italian novelist, was a high-ranking fascist and governor of the province of Novara.

AYOT ST LAWRENCE, WELWYN, HERTS.
STATION: WHEATHAMPSTEAD, G.N.R. 2¼ MILES. 7th March 1927
TELEGRAMS. BERNARD SHAW, CODICOTE.

IO ADELPHI TERRACE. W.C.2.

Povera Molli

Why do you send me such heartbreaking letters without an address to comfort you at ? I wondered sometimes whether you knew that these charming people were incorrigible thieves, shameless ingrates, and infamous cooks, especially the male variety, all spoilt by mean ill usage and insult. A black staff from Georgia would have been better to begin with. *good enough* You must learn to bully them and sack them until you get a collection to become gradually ashamed to rob you, lie to you, cheat you, and ruin your goods by lazy and reckless handling.

I have just had to stop for dinner, which was accompanied on the wireless by a jazz band with a negro, or an American pseudo-negro, singing "Let's all go to Mary's house, Mary's house, Mary's house, Let's all go to Mary's house and have a jolly time". Which is just what I would like to do for the rest of the evening if it were not so far off.

I rather thought Lawrence would want a motor boat. I should have a light row boat as well for Peter to paddle about in, and for a stand-by when the engine was out of order ; but a motor boat, and even one which is a bit of a cruiser to stand up against the squalls that swoop down so suddenly on the lake, is something more than a mere luxury if you can afford it. But why not a telpherage arrangement from your house to Pallanza, so that you could cross in a bucket and be independent of the water ,

I was unspeakably touched by your new script. In your second letter you achived a signature of medieval loveliness. Now you must go on with it. When you come to a museum dont worry about the pictures : you have seen enough of them for the present. Make them trot out their old manuscripts, and the lovely old early Italian books printed when the type and setting of the pages were still founded on the manuscripts. Note the margins, which are half the secret of a well set page. See how they avoided white patches and rivers in the rich black block of letterpress, and how my typewriter has just spoilt this page by spacing irregularly.

Now I must go to bed ; for if I write after dinner I get worry dreams. I nearly worked myself dead last week, and must go easy this one. So this is not a letter, but just a hail to let you know that I am listening. It is desperately difficult for me to write anything but my shop work ; but your letters are always highly appreciated (to put it coldly) here. Charlotte says you are unhappy and must give up vagabondage. But a vagabond has moments.

G.B.S.

The note reads:

It is desperately difficult for me to write anything but my shop work; but your letters are always highly appreciated (to put it coldly) here. Charlotte says you are unhappy and must give up vagabondage. But a vagabond has moments.

G.B.S.

Ayot St Lawrence. Welwyn. Herts. 4th April 1927

Mollemia

Your handwriting is a great success: you must experiment a little further. I have collected

Charlotte says she *does* want them back; but she'll forget.

a set of specimens for you, which you need not send back. I think Vincentano & Michael Angelo

have the best of it. You must acquire that final grace.

I assure you I didn't write Lewis's play. He will develop all right. He and his Dooshka

have been here today for the first time.

Where is Lawrence? Are you still alone with the boy and the big dog? What is the lake

like in April?

Yes: the book is finished: that is, I sent the last sheet of copy to the printer a week

or so ago. There is still all the proof correction to be done. I want a design for it. Eric

Kennington has undertaken to try his hand. A hollow laugh burst from me when I read your figure of 18,000 ~~pages~~ words. The truth is at least 190,000 words. It has been a stupendous job; and I am not at all sure that it is not mere senile drivel. I miss from its babytalk the sweep of my ancient periods. "Ah, where is the spell that once hung on my numbers?"

Have you a wireless set? Are you really utterly unmusical? Life without all Beethoven's symphonies and Mozart's operas and Handel's Messiah and Bach's B minor Mass in one's head must funny, to say nothing of Wagner.

I once saw a colossal Roman daughter by Rubens sold at Christie's for £300, and then a Phillips for £11,000. A horrid subject, but only because the father is old, and a father. Like me, alas!

G. B. S.

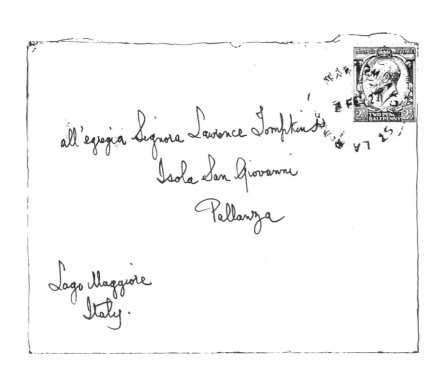

all'egregia Signora Lawrence Tompkins
Isola San Giovanni
Pallanza

Lago Maggiore
Italy.

I have just received this from the wife of the Poet Laureate. I send it to you (I don't want it back) as a specimen of deliberately acquired artistic handwriting founded on the best old Italian models. It is the sort of thing that Higgins taught

G. Bernard Shaw Esq

Ayot St Lawrence,

Welwyn

Herts —

Telegrams: Boars Hill. From **Mrs R BRIDGES,**
Station: Oxford, 5 Miles. Chilswell, near Oxford.

R. B. asks me to let you know that we find — on enquiry at the Clarendon Press — that all the S.P.E. tracts (up to the last, issued a few weeks ago) have been duly posted to you at 10 Adelphi Terrace —   Tract x, which he wanted you to see, is being sent to you addressed to Ayot St Lawrence. He thinks you may like to hear that we now have 260 names on the list of S.P.E. members —
We are hoping for another chance to see you & Mrs Shaw on this hill some day this summer.

May 14.   M. M. B.

Kelmscott Manor
Lechlade, Gloucestershire

Feb. 28: 1927

My dear Shaw
　　　Thank you ever so much
for your cheque, for which I enclose
a formal receipt. . Also thanks
for advice: Yes, Lord Olivier's & Clynes
names are already added, and I was
waiting to ask MacDonald till he
got over his holiday in the winter.
Yes I agree about the advisability
of not scaring a certain class of
people away. We also have Hardy
& I shall ask the others probably.
　　　I saw the show of drawings &c
for the Lawrence Book and was
much interested by Kennington's Arab
portraits, and disliked wholly

The other man's would be imaginative-decorative bits — Hughes-Stanton, wasn't it? I must try to see the book which I want to read. Those portraits are the 'real thing' and give one a ~~sort~~ glimpse of the desert

Yours   May. Morris

This is another specimen of May Morris's writing. Her father, William Morris (the great W. M.) gave her a sixteenth century Italian book by Vincentino; and from that she learnt how to write (having previously, I believe, written in the Red Gulch manner).

What do you think of this for a handwriting? The lady is old enough to be your mother (though I cannot see her that way) and her hand is not so firm as it once was; but this is the way Higgins taught Eliza to write in the play. It is a beautiful acquired Italian handwriting; and when I look at it I wonder I can bear your Red Gulch scrawl, which might without losing its character become beautiful too.

Tear this up. — Nov. 24: 1926.

My dear Shaw

Will you let me put your name down on the General Committee of the Memorial Hall at Kelmscott? It will not let you in for any work, but I shall be grateful for your support and sympathy. The names on the proof enclosed are those of a few of the friends who have consented: but I have a terrifying list of people I have

> to ask later.
> I have waited year by year for
> better times for asking for money—
> but why wait longer for what
> doesn't come₁? *the times, I mean.* And yet, good
> times or bad times, people can
> always find their thousands
> for a Michelham Sale!
>   Yours always sincerely
>   May. Morris

The note at the top of the handwriting sample reads:

What do you think of this for a handwriting? The lady is old enough to be your mother (though **I** cannot see her that way) and her hand is not so firm as it once was; but this is the way Higgins taught Eliza to write in the play. It is a beautiful acquired Italian handwriting; and when I look at it I wonder I can bear your Red Gulch scrawl, which might without losing its character become beautiful too.
Tear this up.   G.B.S.

TELEGRAMS

SOCIALIST, PARL-LONDON.

4, WHITEHALL COURT,

LONDON.S.W.1.

5th November 1927

My dear Molly

    Do they teach the Ballillas anything but a little drill and how
to shout Viva il Duce!? My reason for asking is that the people who
established the Boy Scouts in Italy before the war complain that when
they were broken up by Black Shirts to the cry of Al Morte gli Esplo-
ratori and replaced by the Ballillas all attempt to teach them anything was dropped. I have raised a tremendous dust here by certain
letters of mine which have been published; and this question has aris-
en among others. What was the experience of Tompkinsetto?

    I had really a dreadful time in Stresa. I had to preserve the
dignity of Mrs Shaw and Mr Tompkins (to say nothing of my own before
all the world) as well as the character of Mrs Tompkins, who was determined to throw it away and lead me captive. Mrs Shaw, though resolu-
tely kind, was naturally uneasy; Mr Tompkins was angelic but a helpless prisoner on an island; Mrs Tompkins was possessed by seventy and
seven devils in addition to being xxxxx the very devil herself. But
Troubeskoy and Coates I should have bolted after the first week of
storms.

    I wonder does she ever feel any remorse.

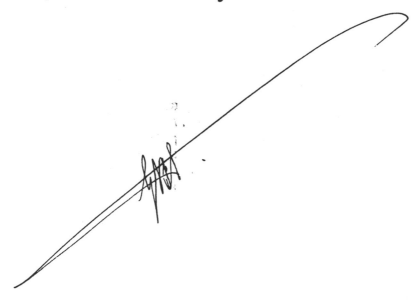

c/o the Viscount Astor
Cleveden, Taplow
8th Jan. 1928

My dear Mrs. Tompkins

I have to thank you for your kind and informative reply to my inquiry concerning the Ballyhooleys.

We have been snowed up in this famous countryhouse since Xmas eve. We leave tomorrow; but I use the address because I would have you know that the Isolino and its chatelaine are not the only pebbles on the beach.

Further, Lady Astor is a devotee of Christian Science. One day, when we were discussing it, I told her the story of the American lady who sat behind me at Kings College on a celebrated occasion, hating me horribly, and how when I rose to go away I found my spine all rusty and my occiput grating on it, so that I was ill for 30 days, and then recovered suddenly and miraculously. Lady Astor and her guest Mrs. Tennant, an eminent exponent and practitioner of Christian Science, had no doubt whatever that the American lady's hatred had blasted and bewitched my spine: such happenings were commonplace to them.

Then I began to think. For there is another American lady who loved me, and then gave me a shock by looking at me with hatred in her eyes and speaking with it in her voice. I nearly ran back to London (we were in Italy); but I unfortunately could not obey this salutary impulse. And, as I now remember, I presently got ill, in spite of swimming and sunbathing. And I cannot get really well, as I was the year before, when the heavens were void of hatred. That wicked woman is giving me absent treatments of hatred. Perhaps she has made a wax figure of me and is sticking pins into it, like Sister Helen. Only by casting her out utterly can I escape the spell; and I find that somehow I cannot do that. The old tenderness gives the witch her grip; and I languish and must presently die of her hatred. Unless she relents and sends a message of love I am a lost man, though a most innocent one. Innocent or not, her adoration was an indispensable Vitamin in my bread of life; and if I perish my blood will be upon her head.

So that is how I am inside, though externally I "peacock" here (Charlotte's expression) amid week end crowds of visitors. Except for this funny Xmas episode I have no news. The book is finished and will appear as soon as its index and chapter headings go to press.

How is Lawrence? And how is his malignant merciless wife? Did the great snowstorm reach you on the lake? Did the boy come home for Xmas? and was he much changed by his prison? you must relieve my uneasy soul by a sign of life.
                                                                        GBS

Though Shaw did not know it, M.T. was at that moment writing a play with Shaw as a character, in which she did worse than "sticking pins" in his image. P.T. had been put in La Villa, a boarding school in Lausanne.

124

2ⁿᵈ March 1928

4, WHITEHALL COURT, LONDON, S.W.1.

If you could see the desert of my correspondence you would not grudge me its few flowers. Write oftener, far oftener, even if I cannot answer. The restless hands sometimes tire of the pen and remember the road to Baveno.

The vision is not quite right. This place is rather wonderful at night with its feet in the skies and its panorama of the river from St Paul's to Westminster. When the roads are black wet, and the embankment lights and car headlights are pouring floods of gold down them, there is really nothing like it in the world. I am alone tonight (Charlotte in the country); and if you would just ring at the door ——.

Well, I will write as soon as I can; but I am being osteopathed for neuritis in my writing arm; and I am more to be written to than made to write. Do not lose faith.

G.B.S.

From their Adam house on Adelphi Terrace, which was being torn down, the Shaws had just moved a few blocks up the Thames to a vast Victorian apartment house at Whitehall Court.

Oakwood Park Hotel
Conway, N. Wales
7th April 1928

My dear Molly,

I have finished the play for you in such a way as to cancel all your false tragedy (Lawrence, I presume, *hasn't* drowned himself) and produce an innocuous and amusing ending. Whether it will prove a happy one remains to be seen. You may write Italian opera and romantic tragedy or you may write studies of modern life; but you must not attempt to combine the two. A mixture of Tosca and Trovatore with Tchekoff is ridiculous: false beauty and bitter truth flourish apart but not together.

The stage device of entering at the back and overhearing, childish as it is, is still effective if not too crudely used. But when you use it baldly three times in a three-act play, and would evidently use it without a blush five times in a five-act one, can you expect the audience to keep its countenance? You must be a little more inventive than that.

Your dialogue is easy and good; you have an eye for character; and there are one or two strokes in the action that shew some subtlety and promise. But you have only one subject. And you are still a terrible savage. Possibly on reading this you will give up in despair, as you did when your first daubs failed to affect me like masterpieces by Monet; but I can't help that.

You really must not write furious letters to your unfortunate boy's schoolmasters complaining that he cannot spell. The result will be that they will waste his time and brains and make him miserable by trying to force him to memorize sets of letters without success. It is a sign of intelligence not to spell conventionally and to spell phonetically. Our spelling, like French spelling, can be acquired only by eye-memory: he will pick it up from reading, or else, like Napoleon, Sheridan, and many other able persons he will never pick it up at all, and will get on quite well without it.

During the quiet winter months on the island, as a catharsis from the emotional events of the summer, M.T. had finished the play (set on Lake Maggiore with three protagonists and a hero who leaps from a parapet to be drowned in the lake) and sent it to Shaw.

I greatly approve of his telling you you ought to be ashamed of yourself when you told him that slaves had no reason to complain because they shared the kindnesses of the hearthrug dogs. But the extent to which your way of life has corrupted him comes out in his proposal to make Angelo's son his servant. Tell him to be civil to Angelo junior, as it is quite possible that the youth may become a Henry Ford, and Peter his hard-up employee. "Service is no inheritance" nowadays.

We are Easter-holidaying here for the moment.

Your beautiful Italian handwriting is changing into unintelligible signs. You must go over your alphabet and correct it until no letter in it can possibly be mistaken for another. Your s's and bs and ts are drifting into the same scrawl; and the ms and Greek es require attention.

I write in great haste, the finishing of the play having left me no time to catch this Saturday post, or to make myself in the very least agreeable.

My book on Socialism will soon be out now. It will amuse me to find out whether you can read it.

On the subject of *la guerra,* read Kenworthy's "Will Civilization Crash?" It will explain to you the danger of war with America.

à te—

G.B.S.

The original play, with its third act completely written over in red ink by Shaw, was unfortunately lost; no copies had been made.

Dearest Molly

I forgot the title. It should be Triangoli Intrecciati—Interlaced Triangles; and the scene should be described as Villa on Lago Peggiore. How to classify it puzzles me: an Opera without Music would do very well. Basile must translate it, using the Baronessa as his dictionary. Then get it typed in proper form and give it to Cesare Castelli, Vio Cimabue 3, Milano, to place for you, unless you or the Baron have enough knowledge of the Italian theatres to dispense with an agent. Castelli is my agent. The play is not at all impossible theatrically if an actress can be found for it who is fascinating enough to prevent Carlotta from being simply odious.

Don't tell Castelli, or anyone but your nearest and dearest, that *I* spoilt your play. You have had your revenge; for I have had two days horrid headache following the outrage.

GBS

31st May 1928
chez Lady Astor at Restharrow
(O gelosia!)

My dear Mollikins

All you have to do is to tell Mr. William Foyle, bookseller, Charing Cross Road, London W.C. 2 that you have an original edition of the Guide with the author's autograph, and that you want to exchange it for a clean copy and thirty guineas, and the thing is done.

Henry is right as to the island. It is a place to spend six weeks a year in, but not a place to live in. You have no business there—no roots in it. The life you are leading is horribly wicked. You cannot keep blasting your soul without blasting your body as well; that is what is the matter with your lungs; the warning colds will develop into tuberculosis, accelerated by drugs and self-hatred; and you will perish miserable. I can do nothing. Other American women save themselves by Christian Science, public work, motherhood (called matriarching by Storm Jameson) and not being prettier than they can help. But you are a predestinate damned soul, a Vamp fiend, neither doing justice, loving mercy, nor walking humbly with your God. You will prowl round that lake, making men's wives miserable, tormenting yourself whenever their glances wander from you for a moment, until the lake water changes to fire and brimstone and rises up and scorches you into nothingness.

Lawrence works and fences; Troubetskoy sculpts; Albert and Cecil work like negroes and have no use for women who do not work; Basile overworks and has married a gentlewoman who will hold him when he will post policemen to whistle when you are coming so that he may fly; but *you*—what do you do? what will become of you? how will you face old age: With a "lifted" face, with grease paints and an iceball and rouge, with peroxided hair, an old hag desperately pretending to be a young witch. Oh Molly, Molly, Molly, Molly, I must not think about you; for I cannot save you; I have done my best and only made matters worse.

Can you not learn how to live in the world: You are not a thing evil in itself; and it is impossible to believe that you *must* go to the devil by natural necessity, though my experience tells me that you will. For Mephistopheles whispers to me as he did to Faust "She is not the first." Before you were born I have had to do with sirens as seductive as you. And now! You will go their way unless you can relegate love affairs to very occasional distractions, and then not spend more than an hour a fortnight or so on them. What sort of creature do you suppose I should be now if I had done nothing but exploit my celebrated fascination all my life? Would you have looked twice at so repulsive an object? And yet you thought that when you had secured your Ogygia and lured me to its shores you could play Calypso to me Odysseus and make a hog of me. Aren't you glad you didn't succeed: After all, you have some brains in your upper half. This erotic-romantic attitude to life doesn't make you happy.

If only you had a sense of humor! You could write plays if you had.

I have no use for a woman who can't laugh at herself.

Your spiritual values are all wrong.

It seems such a pitiful waste—a woman of quite considerable capacity and vitality thrown on the scrap heap for want of one trifling ingredient, and because some fool invented looking glasses.

Well, I am not going to start another sheet. Besides, the hostess calls; some social game or other is in hand

a te, O cara
GBS

The guide is *The Intelligent Woman's Guide to Socialism,* a dedicated first edition of which Shaw sent to M.T. but that she found dreadfully boring.

HOTEL BEAU-SITE

NINO'S RESTAURANT

CAP D'ANTIBES

3rd Sept. 1928.

My dear Molly

For seven weeks I have been hiding within a day's ride of your Renaud. I shall have left when this reaches you.

I enclose a press cutting to make you jealous.

I am not in the least angry: why should I be? But you should not drive me away to horrible hell-paradises like the Riviera by refusing to behave yourself tactfully.

In this place when you are not bathing or driving over the mountains you are stark mad with irritable despair. We arrived in the

middle of the heat wave in July, and could not
get Réginesque accommodation. The first four or five
weeks were terrible.

All your fault.

Signora Lawrence Josephkins
Isola San Giovanni
Pallanza
Lago Maggiore

Italie

AYOT ST LAWRENCE, WELWYN, HERTS.
STATION:WHEATHAMPSTEAD,L.&N.E.R.2¼ MILES.
TELEGRAMS:BERNARD SHAW, CODICOTE.

2nd February 1929.

unpossessed?

4,WHITEHALL COURT, LONDON, S.W.1.

Dearest Mollikins

How Rome? Wherefore the Palazzo Orsini? What about San Giovanni? Is the chair empty, is the sword unswayed, the island unnnnnnnd? Do you forget that I know nothing except what I pick up when gossiping with Cecil Lewis?

Who is Carlo? Is he Basile? Have you run away from Lawrence with him to Rome? Are they making the boy a good Rosminian Catholic in that seminary where they told me proudly that every boy had a whole bath once a fortnight? Cecil told me that when I sent you those ridiculous reports that I had bought an island you believed them. This proves that if you only live on an island of that size long enough you become an idiot.

You desire to know whether I am Thru with you. At my age one is thru with everybody, and can only beg for a little charitable tolerance from young persons. I hoarded my bodily possessions so penuriously that even at seventy I had some left; but that remnant was stolen from me on the road to Baveno and on other roads to paradise through the same district. Now they are all dusty highways on which I am safe because nobody can rob a beggar. Nothing is left except my eternal genius. When that endless book was finished (the one you took as a personal insult) I thought I was finished; but when Barry Jackson announced a festival of my plays at Malvern in August next, with nothing newer than Joan and Methuselah and Heartbreak House, I erupted like a volcano and simply hurled out a new play, inspiringly entitled The Apple Cart. As it is all about politics except for twenty minutes in the middle between a He Man and a She Woman of my patent brand, perhaps it will interest you. I sent you -- or intended to send you -- the newspaper pictures of Pola Negri and G.B.S., just to shew you that if you come to Vamping you are not the only pebble on the beach. But really the lady was quite nice and modest and simply dressed, and made no attempt to wake the dead.

That is all my news. You have seen it all in the papers, probably. I gather that there are moments when your thoughts (or dreams) turn to me ; and I am glad that there is still something immortal for you to turn to. It is hard for me to write letters now ; but I can always read them when the Italian postmark is on them.

Rome is a magical place. When I was there I knew I had been there in a *former existence. And so, with this touch of my own hand — though of course all before has been tapped out by me — ever, G.B.S.*

The note reads:

. . . former existence. And so, with this touch of my own hand—though of course all before has been tapped out by me—

 ever, G.B.S.

When it became too damp and cold on the Isolino, M.T. rented a flat in the Duchess of Sermoneta's palazzo in Rome in which to spend the winter months.

132

Ayot St Lawrence, Welwyn, Herts. 2/4/29

This is what I looked like when I saw that dreadful picture. How had you the heart to send it to me? And the others! What a crew! Va, perdutissima!

Signora Lawrence Langner
Villa Orani

The picture referred to is a mystery, though it may have been a reproduction of one of M.T.'s first serious attempts at painting.

You really <u>are</u> a duffer — couldn't even poison yourself properly!

There is nothing wrong with your glands: what you need, too attractive one, is a job in a factory without anything but your wages to live on and dress on: all the better if you had to support the boy into the bargain.

What Lawrence needs is, first, a divorce, and then a placid but efficient cook-housekeeper-wife to take care of him. He will be surprised to find how pleasant domestic happiness is.

I trust nobody in the Palazzo can read English. To undertake a letter is impossible: I have not a moment. Besides, all these commonplaces of an idle life have no importance except to their victims.

G.B.S.

AYOT ST LAWRENCE, WELWYN, HERTS. 10ᵗʰ April 1929

STATION: WHEATHAMPSTEAD, L. & N.E.R. 2¼ MILES.

TELEGRAMS: BERNARD SHAW, CODICOTE.

4, WHITEHALL COURT, LONDON, S.W.1.

16th August 1929

Telephone No. 338.

Telegraphic Address:
Malvern Hotel, Malvern.

Malvern Hotel,

Malvern.

Molly, Molly,

For heavens sake be careful: that's not genius: it's veronal. I know a lady who believes herself to be the greatest violinist in the world, and communes daily with the spirit of Mozart, cutting all her family dead.

However, perhaps she is happy. Only, that ghastly sort of happiness sometimes turns to the most desolating wretchedness as a preliminary to despair, fury, and death.

I did not tell you to stop painting: why should I? I told you to work away at it for ten years. But the tearful shock of not being told that your bright little daub was a masterpiece for surpassing Monets best was too much for you. Do you still seriously think that it _was_.

Come! I'll give you a commission. £5 for a competently painted picture of your house, not more than 15" square. +50 lire! Must be a sound trade article which I can exhibit without spoiling the room.

I was in Italy — Jugo Slavia from the middle of April to the middle of June, and saw the isola from the train window both going and coming.

I was 73 last month. An awful old man.

29th April 1930.
4, WHITEHALL COURT LONDON, S.W.1.

But where? and have you received the letter I sent you the other day to Rome?

You hurl a letter from a Milan hotel, without place, name, or circumstance, and expect me to turn up in my best clothes, catalogue in hand, to adore your infamous masterpieces!

You have lost the light of reason. Be more explicit, tesoro!

Carlo Borelli, editor of the *Corriere della Sera,* arranged for M.T. to have a one-man show of her paintings at the Galleria Brera in Milan. It was well reviewed and sold several pictures.

Mollimolli

I have worked seven days a week for the last six months at the horrible drudgery of compiling a Collected Edition of all my works; and now my machinery has stopped dead and left me with a few days holiday to write nonsense.

Easter Sunday, 1930.
at Charlotte's sisters widower's, General Hugh Cholmondeley's, en route for the Palace Hotel, Buxton, until the 27th April

EDSTASTON,
WEM,
SALOP.
Derbyshire
TEL.

Peter's conduct seems to me most promising. He has my hearty moral support in his refusal to be imprisoned and made an intellectual and moral imbecile merely to prevent him from bothering you with his importunate relationship. When he is a finished stonemason God can make him a sculptor if he will.

Jung should not get interested in a case so obvious as yours. Give him these notes to copy. "Mary Tompkins. Young American savage. Found on attaining adolescence that she attracted men irresistibly. Was thus in the position of a young male savage coming into a fortune of several billions, or of the fiddler Nero finding himself a Caesar. Being quite untrained for such a

As it was impossible to keep P.T. from playing hooky from any of the various schools into which he was put, L.T. agreed to the experiment of letting him learn a trade by being an apprentice to a sculptor.

destiny became a beggar on horseback; but having a strong head, kept her
seat. All the symptoms pretty bad: ungovernable, cruel, unscrupulous, unmusical, spendthrift, bad mother, ruinous wife, so accustomed to adulation that
she mistakes her crudest daubs for Monet masterpieces and Goya triumphs.
Sole redeeming feature an interest in old Shaw difficult to reconcile with her
general depravity, but probably a relic of innate inherited good taste. Not worth
bothering about: must concentrate on husband who is throwing himself away on
her."

There! I have not wholly neglected you all these centuries: Cecil Lewes
has kept me supplied with news. He has just returned to Maggiore.
Sympathetic regards to Lawrence. Nothing for you that you would care for. I'm 73¾
G.B.S.

Before suggesting to M.T. that she make a
career of painting in order to cure the depres-
sion that had led her to an attempted suicide,
L.T. had taken her to Zurich to consult Professor Jung.

138

The Malvern Hotel, 21st Sept. 1930

My dentist's address (for which, dear Molliken, you never asked me) is J. A. Holden, 40 Park Lane, London W. 1. He is American.

As far as I can judge from black & white photographs your case as a painter is by no means hopeless. Your personal combination of striking qualities and infamous defects is reflected in it. You have a very just perception of the significant aspects of what you see: for instance that postcard picture of your house is so right in its values that it is not only instantly recognizable (a photograph might be that) but produces the effect of the place on the imagination. In handling a figure you can model it extraordinarily well: one can almost feel the flesh as well as see it. There is no niggling: your masses are courageously right. I cannot see the color; but I guess it as rich and deeply felt. These qualities, with your good looks and insensate energy, explain your rapid and easy conquest of the London and Milanese exhibitors. But they will not carry you all the way, because you have not only obvious faults of execution but frightful counterqualities, not to say vices. To begin with the simplest and most obvious, you wont draw. I dont say you can't draw; for the rapid success with which you changed your abominable handwriting convinced me that you can do what you like with your fingers. But you are content to be a blobber (more politely, an Impressionist); and there are things in nature that cannot be blobbed: they must be drawn. It is no use modelling a torso perfectly and then putting beside it a swan that looks like nothing but the old property swan used at the first performance of Lohengrin and used as a Teddy Bear by countless generations of puppies ever since. Swans must be drawn and serpents must be drawn. They have beauty and whip of line: their life is in that line: in fact they have hardly anything else. If you make them look like bags of cotton waste, and leaky bags at that, you betray a blind spot in your artistic perception which is instantly and most offensively obvious to the least critical spectator. Therefore you must spend an hour a day for the next six months at pen drawing: drawing butterflies daddy-long-legses, grasshoppers in scientific lepidopterous detail, also flowers and fishes, until you can draw fairies with perfect daintiness and elegance of line.

140

But there is something deeper than this. Absence of drawing is mere slovenly want of conscience resulting in a low standard of draughtsmanship. But there is something positive the matter. When you deal with human subjects your taste is depraved, wicked, beastly. You should take in a French Nudist magazine called La Vie Intégrale and think seriously about the effect of clothes on the figure. If an Italian contadina (or a Venetian Renaissance courtesan for that matter) heaps herself with heavy petticoats and skirts and never changes them, never airs or suns herself, she has only to be stripped to reveal herself as a most repulsive pile of flesh. To strip her is simply indecent: if you paint her you must paint her clothes, not the degraded lump they hide. Until you feel this, and cannot bear to shew the human figure except in its healthy natural beauty your nudes will always be disgusting. A fine natural figure always has delicious drawing in it: that is why people who cannot draw, but who have a sense of beauty, always want to get their hands on you. Think about it, Molly: cultivate your taste: leave Red Gulch behind you; and angels will always love you, including

G.B.S.

See what inexorable Time has done
    You that have beauty still
Waste no regrets : just say
This dog has had his day
    His flesh its fill.
    Turn from the setting to the rising sun
Love bettering men, and let the worsening die
For I, dear Mary, am no longer I.

POST CARD

This space for communication

The address to be written here

Ayot St Lawrence
27th January 1931.

Portrait by
OLIVE EDIS, F.R.P.S.
SHERINGHAM

The sixth and seventh lines read:

Turn from the setting to the rising sun
Love bettering men, and let the
    worsening die

AYOT ST LAWRENCE, WELWYN, HERTS. 7th Feb. 1931   4, WHITEHALL COURT, LONDON, S.W.1.
STATION: WHEATHAMPSTEAD, L.& N.E.R. 2¼ MILES.
TELEGRAMS: BERNARD SHAW, CODICOTE.
TELEPHONE: CODICOTE 18.

No: nothing wrong; but I was touched by your letter, and yet felt that you were thinking of a younger man and had better be prepared for the inevitable shock of our next meeting, when perhaps I shall forget the passage of the years.

You see, bellissima, you and Lawrence will still be in the prime of life twenty years hence. There is a horrible possibility that I may be — I will not say what you would call else — but above ground. Have you ever thought of what I shall be like then? Even in ten years I shall be 85, a doddering whistling anecdote repeating old bore. Therefore love me as long as you can; but make young friends: the old ones will wear out long before you are both worn out yourselves. I must have some provident care for you or I would not take the trouble to warn you and shield you from disappointment and disillusion.

Mr Brownrigg telephones he will come up London tomorrow to call on me. Unfortunately I'm not in London and shall not be until Thursday; so he must call on me here or write. I am most desperately pressed to get some work finished before I start on a tour of the Mediterranean on the 4th March to save my life and Charlotte's (we haven't had even a Sunday off for months except for her accident); but of course I can move if a serious necessity arises. You understand, of course, that only Lawrence, or someone invested by Lawrence with legal powers to represent him, can prevail against a schoolmaster who is in loco parentis. He can set aside even you as far as the law is concerned. I do not believe for a moment that Peter can be made a man of in the Etonian sense; and indeed God forbid that he should! He is too much a man already, having always been treated as an adult. However, we shall see as the situation develops. It was pleasant to hear your voice (refined a little by Roman society – eh?); but all the lessons in articulation you had in Gower St and from Mouldy Mackenzie are forgotten, and I could hardly catch ten words

AYOT ST LAWRENCE, WELWYN, HERTS.
STATION: WHEATHAMPSTEAD. L. & N.E.R. 2¼ MILES.
TELEGRAMS: BERNARD SHAW, CODICOTE.
16 Feb 1931
4, WHITEHALL COURT, LONDON. W.

Norman G. Brownrigg was headmaster of Fernden, the English prep school in Surrey to which P.T. had been sent but in which they were having a hard time keeping him.

144

A long letter from Norman Brownrigg impresses me favorably. I have made an appointment with him for Thursday, and will then write more fully. I shall be at Whitehall from Thursday morning to Saturday midday.

Meanwhile your friend Osborne, who did not call on me, had better stop writing to Peter, who, N.B. says, is "quite fit and jolly."

The real danger is that N.B. may get fed up and send Peter home as an undesirable. That would be serious. His truancies in Italy and Switzerland do not matter; but anything savoring of expulsion from a public school or a good preparatory one in England would put a black mark against him that must be avoided at all costs.

How old is Peter? I am terribly at a loss through my ignorance of his age. However, never mind: N.B. will tell me.

G.B.S.

4, WHITEHALL COURT, LONDON, S.W.1.

·AYOT ST LAWRENCE, WELWYN, HERTS. 17th Feb. 1931
STATION: WHEATHAMPSTEAD. L.&N.E.R. 2¼ MILES.
TELEGRAMS: BERNARD SHAW, CODICOTE.

P.T. was eleven years old.

With Bernard Shaw's compliments

Send your diplomatist along: I had forgotten
all about him, being badly overworked just now.

Ayot St. Lawrence, Welwyn, Herts.

27/1/31.

AYOT ST LAWRENCE, WELWYN, HERTS. 17ᵗʰ Feb. 1931
STATION: WHEATHAMPSTEAD, L.& N.E.R. 2¼ MILES.
TELEGRAMS: BERNARD SHAW, CODICOTE.
TELEPHONE: CODICOTE 18.

4, WHITEHALL COURT, LONDON, S.W.I.

My dear Molly

This isn't about Peter, as I shall not see N.B. until tomorrow.

When you meet the Granville-Barkers don't mention me in her presence, as
you will embarrass him and infuriate her. She hates me with a lethal malignity
which seriously damages my health if I come near her; and if by
disregarding her feelings you draw any of that hatred on yourself you may
not only suffer in the same way but will certainly lose the interesting acquaintance of G-B.
She has detached him entirely from me. Lawrence's devotion to you is feeble compared to
his to her; and he has thought the world well lost for her — and lost it, because
though she has quite serious literary talent she has not an idea in her head later than
1865, and quite honestly believed that, in getting him away from his old associates she
was redeeming him socially and artistically. He was a playwright in the running with

myself: now he is almost forgotten. The Labor Party would probably have made him a peer (they were desperately hard up for presentable men who could afford to enter the House of Lords) if he had stuck to his Fabian politics. In 20 years he has produced only two plays. One is no use: the other I have tried to persuade Barry Jackson to produce at the Malvern Festival; so far in vain; but I have hopes. I tried to get him knighted (to please her) at the last distribution of honors; but as he dropped the Labor Party it naturally dropped him.

So be careful how you tread. Do not broach the sore subject of G.B.S. But if you can let me have any news of him it will interest me. He has an Italian strain in him and was meant to be a man of genius.

Whatever you do, don't call her Mrs Barker. She insists on the hyphenation.

In haste for the village post.

From Bernard Shaw.

4, WHITEHALL COURT (130) LONDON, S.W.1.
PHONE: VICTORIA 3160.
TELEGRAMS: SOCIALIST. PARL-LONDON.

19th February
1931

My dear Molly

You will see by the enclosed that the interview had been upset by the act of God. Mr Brownrigg wants me to go down to see the school, which will convince you thst he is quite willing to let me see Peter; but there are two difficulties. First, it will take me a whole day, which I cannot spare this week, as I start for a trip round the Mediterranean on the 4th, and have a frightful lot of things to arrange or finish before I leave. Second and more serious, I fear that the effect of a visit on Peter would be to unsettle him again just as he is getting into his stride as a boxer, chess player, and British schoolboy. It is this last consideration which really prevents me from throwing over everything for a trip to Haslemere.

Let me fire off a few general propositions for your pondering.

Nobody can make a man of Peter from the outside. He must make a man of himself : all you or N.B. can do is to give him a chance. The best conclusion I can come to is that N.B. and Haslemere can give him a better chance than you and Rome. You know that I am the enemy of the school system : I may be said to be the discoverer of the glaring fact that schools are prisons into which children are locked to prevent them worrying their parents. But that does not alter the hard fact that there is at present no organization of child life as such : there is nothing but the family, the school, or the streets. The family, plus the day school, is the best, provided the family is big enough, with sisters and brothers in it. But the one-child family is the very devil if the parents are not Mr and Mrs Ruskin, orderly and pious, but Molly and Lawrence. Peter is between it and Haslemere or vagrancy ; and can you doubt that Haslemere is best ?

Also you must stop writing whatever comes into your head to Peter. A correspondence of that kind between a married woman and a schoolboy is not any the less unsuitable and morbid because they happen to be mother and son. It is extremely lucky that he has stopped writing to you. Dont recommence the correspondence. A very occasional and not too unnaturally stiff duty-letter will be quite sufficient. Cut the apron string, and cut it for ever. If you want to express yourself in heart-to-heart correspondence, write to ME.

And never write to a schoolmaster. If you dont trust him to the extent of believing that the boy is better in his sdhool than at home, take him home. If you leave him at school dont drive the master mad. Peter must take his chance with the rest. I lately had

to do with a ~~correscpondence~~ between *a boy's mother and* the headmaster of one of
the English public schools ; an~~d~~ the man was beyond description :
I would not have put a hedgehog in his ca~~s~~e. I therefore know
what a typical headmaster (I am afraid he <u>was</u> typical) can be.
N.B. is an angel and a Savior by contrast w<u>i</u>th him. N.B. seems to
be as good as Peter has the least chance of finding. And he sees
through Peter's acting, which is very important, as he will neither punish it as if it were serious delinque~~n~~cy nor encourage ,
it by being taken in by it. He dismisses the run-away as Peters
little attempt to live up dramatically to his reputation. The al-
leged exploits at the police station are obviously touches of romance.

    In short, do nothing except choke off Mr Osborne. Let Peter
alone. Let N.B. alone. Nothing dreadful will happen until Peter
comes back trained, and objects strenuously and snobbishly to .
your way of life as bad form. I do not mean that he will ever be
a conventional routine bourgeois : no doubt he will be an artist
and possibly an immoral and revolutionary one. But he will not be
a young blackguard shocking Cecil Lewis by using language to you,
not that no son should address to his mother, but that no gentlem~~a~~
could address to a comparatively elderly lady.

    I must post this and go to bed. I am giving you the best
advice I can : give it the best consideration you can. If you decide to take it, dismiss the matter from your mind and tell me all
about the Granville-Barkers and Fanny's First Play.

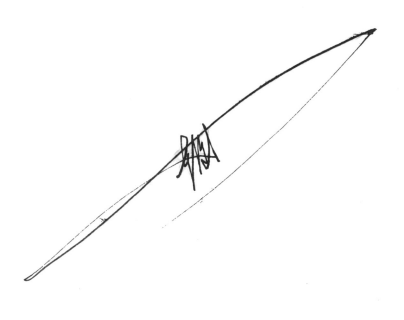

Ayot St. Lawrence, Welwyn, Herts.
Station: Wheathampstead, L. & N.E.R. 2¼ miles.
Telegrams: Bernard Shaw, Codicote.
Telephone: Codicote 18.

4, Whitehall Court,
London, S.W. 1

15th July 1931

Dear Mollikins

I can't take anyone to Russia, not even my wife. Madelon and Albert tell me that unmentionable horrors will destroy me if I go; but they spoil it all by proposing that I shall join them there when the Opera is in full blast.

Did you really live in a square when you were a child? I am disappointed: I pictured a cave, or at least a wigwam.

Mr. Brownrigg invited me to his school breaking-up; but I could not go. He seems hopeful of making Peter that wonder of the world: a British Schoolboy. I gather that the said Wonder runs away quite seldom now.

Have you learnt to draw yet? Swans, for instance?

You turn up bewilderingly on the Isola after settling in Rome and telling me that you could no longer afford lacustrine dwellings. Have you renewed your lease?

Have you not yet discovered that the only roads that remain beautiful are those that never led anywhere? For you never come to the end of them.

I start on Saturday and shall have no fixed address until next month.

GBS

Obliged by the 1929 crash to give up the Isolino as well as the apartment in Rome, M.T., after dismantling the house on the island and putting the furniture up for auction, had suggested going to Russia with Shaw.

Malvern. 13th Aug. 1931

My dear Molly

Have the Italian papers reported me as disappointed with Russia and unhappy about it? If so, their mendacity is colossal. Here the scandal is that I am boosting Russia to the skies: my visit now seems like an extraordinarily jolly dream: never in my life have I enjoyed a journey so much. You would have been disgusted at my reception as a Grand Old Man of Socialism, my smilings and wavings and posings and speech makings; but it made things very smooth for us all.

I could not have taken you with me, as the party was a political one into which you would not have fitted, as you are not a political animal. It consisted of Lord and Lady Astor and their son David Astor, and the Marquess of Lowthian. We are all deeply and conscientiously interested in social conditions and have religions of our own and are affectionate friends. Charles Tennant, who was also with us, is a Christian Scientist. In short, we were the sort of party that you could not even conceive, as you waste all your brains (and you have some) on art and erotics.

Ireland can be extraordinarily beautiful, with colors beyond Italian ones, and what Italy often lacks: atmosphere. The climate is much milder than in England; but January is January there as elsewhere. Try the autumn. But though in a picture gallery I can pick out an Irish landscape at a glance, Ireland in its full range of light and color is unpaintable, the scale is too great.

Your drawing is greatly improved: you are really beginning to get a workmanlike line. But your mind is still barbarous: you do not ennoble what you touch. And though I have seen a calf with two heads, a nude gentleman with double organs surprises me. You should be careful not to produce these accidental illusions.

I must stop. I have much to write (for print) about Russia.

GBS

AYOT ST LAWRENCE, WELWYN, HERTS.
STATION: WHEATHAMPSTEAD, L.& N.E.R. 2¼ MILES.
TELEGRAMS: BERNARD SHAW, CODICOTE.
TELEPHONE: CODICOTE 18.

4, WHITEHALL COURT, LONDON, S.W.1.

My dear Molly

How terrifying! What on earth am I to do with you?

Explain, explain, explain. Is Lawrence with you? Have you eloped with the owner of the house? How long are you staying? Have you come for a one-woman show at the galleries or what? How? what? I must know all about it before I can break the devastating news to Charlotte and arrange something.

I shall not be in town until Thursday. Let me have a line here by return.

In great haste

sempre a te

In November of 1931 M.T. arrived in London with thirty-five paintings for a one-woman exhibition at the Leicester Galleries. Of the pictures fourteen were sold and after the show she stayed on for three months painting portraits.

Ayot St Lawrence, Welwyn, Herts. 4/11/31

I am crammed with work and engagements tomorrow up to about 4·15; so do not stay in for me before then. After that I will come when I can, — between 4·15 and 5. sometime. I hope you will find me extremely old.

POST CARD
CARTE POSTALE

Communication—Correspondance

Address—Adresse

Mrs Lawrence Langhland
7 Charles St, Cavendish Sqr,
W. 1.

The last sentence reads:

You will find me extremely old.

AYOT ST LAWRENCE, WELWYN, HERTS. 24ᵗʰ Novʳ. 1931   4, WHITEHALL COURT, LONDON, S.W.1.
STATION: WHEATHAMPSTEAD, L.& N.E.R. 2¼ MILES.
TELEGRAMS: BERNARD SHAW, CODICOTE.
TELEPHONE: CODICOTE 18.

My dear Molly

The postage on English letters is, first, a penny no matter what the weight is. Then, in addition to the invariable penny, a halfpenny for every two ounces. This means three halfpence for all ordinary letters. Postcards, a penny.

On letters to America, three halfpence for the first ounce and a penny for every additional ounce.

On letters to Italy &c &c, twopence halfpenny the first ounce and three halfpence for every additional ounce.

For all postcards abroad, three halfpence.

When writing to me, use the enclosed. On Monday to Thursday mornings inclusive I get my letters here (post before 5.30) and open them myself. On

Friday and Saturday Miss Petch opens them at Whitehall Court in spite of any inscriptions to the contrary. After ten years of it nothing that the wildest woman or maddest lunatic could write produced the smallest impression on her.

On Thursday I may have a spare moment round about 5.

—— the past is going —
this is only a fragment

24th November 1931

AYOT ST LAWRENCE, WELWYN, HERTS.
STATION: WHEATHAMPSTEAD, L.& N.E.R. 2¼ MILES.
TELEGRAMS: BERNARD SHAW, CODICOTE.

4, WHITEHALL COURT, LONDON, S.W.I.

My dear Molly

I have just had an hour of hard exercise in the garden with a pickaxe; and as I cannot write with a pickaxe I must write with a machine, my hands being for the moment tuned only to violent operations.

I had to break off my answer to your letter yesterday because all the time available before the post went was taken up with telling you how many stamps to put on your letters. Serve you right for not buying a postal guide: price one shilling and full of the most surprising information.

First I have to thank you for what you said, and need not say again, as I like to be able to shew your letters to Charlotte and to allow them to divert Miss Patch. Old people have to be very careful not to forget that they are old, and that even when young people adore them, to say nothing of when they dont, they may greatly dislike to be touched by them in any but the most grandfatherly or grandmotherly fashion. When you are old you will find yourself watching rather anxiously for the inevitable falling-off in your painting and the equally inevitable moment when old Mrs Tompkins must finally and decisively put off Molly and all her vanities. I have arrived at that stage ; and you must make allowances for it. Also you must remember that, whatever age we may be in fairyland, in prosaic society we are an old man and a young thing, and that to exhibit ourselves in any other relation would be ridiculous and most unbecoming. So do not be angry if I play my part of pantaloon to your columbine with my usual histrionic skill.

I am not inconsistent ; but you do not know the world as well as I do. In a theatre, money comes in through the payboxes : the actress has not to coax it by giving a private performance to each playgoer, which is what a painter has to do. If she takes less than a living wage for her acting and makes up the difference out of her private means she is driving the actresses who have no private means, and with whom she is competing for work, on the streets (or stalls). Therefore I told you that you must not act for less than a living wage, whether in cash or dresses.

A painter (except a house painter working for wages) is in quite a different case. The President of the Royal Academy is, or in my time used to

156

be, privileged to charge £2,000, or rather guineas, for a full dress portrait, to be hung on the line at the summer exhibition. The screever sits on the flags with his cap beside him, and lives on the pennies dropped into it by passers-by who admire his pastels of a lighthouse, half a salmon, and the king. I remember giving a sovereign years ago to a girl just like you who took to screeving.

Between these two extremes there is not any standard price for pictures : you take what you can get. If you can get only five pounds you must acquire skill and speed enough to paint a picture a week and live on £260 a year. So considerable a painter and poet as George Russell added £260 to his income for years in this way.

Messrs Brown & Phillips might possibly take you up and shove you on to their fashionable clients for a year as a marvellous young genius and induce them to shower guineas on you for a season. I have seen that happen again and again ; and the tragedy of the young painter who believed that it would last when the dealers dropped him and he was no longer the fashion was pretty grim. And the general snobbish tradition that painters, as artists and gentlemen (or Ladies) must price their pictures in guineas in sums of two or three or even four figures, has filled the world with desperately impecunious, seedy, borrowing, begging, drinking, drugging, disgraceful, and unspeakably wretched unsuccessful painters who had far better have been screevers. Hence my Woolworth exhibition catalogue. Hence the saying of Tonks : "the painter's place is in the kitchen", uttered at the opening of Rex Whistler's wall paintings at the Tate Gallery, which were done at so much the square foot, like Ford Madox Brown's frescoes in the Manchester Town Hall.

If you are going to support Lawrence and Peter by your brush you must learn to paint a picture in two days, and you must consider your customers' pockets in pricing them, and your customer's tastes and prejudices and drawingroom walls in determining their sizes and subjects. If the customer wants to decorate a bedroom in an Abode of Love he (or she) may require something quite different from the keeper of a boarding house in Tunbridge Wells ; but unless you can turn your hand to supply a market of some kind you cannot live by painting.

And now I have lost the post, again by trying to educate you.

Do not imagine that my busyness is an evasion or an affectation. My working days in London are not like my holidays in Stresa. I am just now badly overworked, and have taken a cabin for the Cape of Good Hope for Xmas

Eve to get some sunshine and recuperation. I shall perhaps hear from you tomorrow morning as to where I can see the pictures. A rivederti. G.B.S.

Messrs Brown & Phillips, owners of the Leicester Galleries, who, when M. T.'s exhibition was over, arranged for her to paint several portraits of prominent Londoners.

With Bernard Shaw's compliments

I will make a desperate effort to look in at this show between 3·30 and 4...

If you use the second form for a friend you must fill in the name. I am overdrawn but friendly and faithful.

4 Whitehall Court, London S.W.1

22/12/31

Shaw would take M.T. to openings of new exhibitions in London. This note was evidently attached to a couple of invitations.

AYOT ST LAWRENCE, WELWYN, HERTS. 1st May 1932

STATION: WHEATHAMPSTEAD, L.& N.E.R. 2¼ MILES.

TELEGRAMS: BERNARD SHAW, CODICOTE.

TELEPHONE: CODICOTE 18.

4, WHITEHALL COURT, LONDON, S.W.1.

Poor Bobo! Poor Molly!

Never forget that dogs are shortlived, and intolerable nuisances on tours, where they will soon be forbidden.

Beautiful women should never have dogs hanging about them. Try a parrot. Parrots are amusing, and never die. You wish they did.

Lawrence has sent me a play in which he has held the mirror up to Nature with results that would entitle you to a divorce in most American States. But it is not at all badly done, if only the subject were tolerable.

How much do I owe you for the picture? Was it five guineas or ten?

G.B.S.

Bobo, short for Bruno di Bramonte, was an enormous pitch-black great Dane, acquired in Milan in 1928, who died from swallowing a nail.

AYOT ST LAWRENCE, WELWYN, HERTS. 8th July 1932

STATION: WHEATHAMPSTEAD, L.& N.E.R. 2¼ MILES.

TELEGRAMS: BERNARD SHAW, CODICOTE.

TELEPHONE: CODICOTE 18.

4, WHITEHALL COURT, LONDON, S.W.I.

Dear Mr. Osborne

You are reckoning without my age, and my wife's age, and our many preoccupations and pensioners. It is a physical impossibility for us to take on Peter, or to let him regard our house as a port in a storm. We are full up; we have one foot in the grave; and we cannot keep as many irons in the fire as we could in our prime.

But even now I have enough spare money to come to the rescue if any really promising opportunity is being lost for want of it. I can't take charge of a boy; but I _can_ sign a cheque. And that is my limit as far as Peter is concerned. And even that is compromised by my conviction that money

With L.T.'s income virtually cut off, worried about the bad effect it would have on P.T. to be removed from school, D'Arcy Osborne, then in England, solicited Shaw's help.

can do much harm and little good if it is given to a young man for nothing. In particular, if it is used to give him a public school and university education it may simply unfit him for independent self-support.

If Peter should develop a turn for scholarship, his doom may be that of an Eton master or university don. In that case he must be nursed up to it at Winchester (where the introduction of a mathematical master was until lately, and probably still is, regarded as partly a daring modernism and partly a deplorable concession to commercial caddishness) and Cambridge or Oxford. On any other ground the Winchester plan seems to me absurd. He ought to learn Spanish and Russian, not Latin and ancient Greek.

Possibly an American university might be indicated if he is to do anything in business in America, as they effect that qualification there.

Is he clever with his hands? Molly says he is; and as she dislikes him she is probably not flattering him.

In haste to catch the village post
G.B.S.

From Bernard Shaw.

4, WHITEHALL COURT (130) LONDON, S.W.1.
PHONE: VICTORIA 3160.
TELEGRAMS: SOCIALIST. PARL-LONDON.

26th October 1932; *but this must wait until I get your address from Cecil Lewis, who says you are back in Rome.*

My dear Molly

Make a careful note that even the most interesting and heart-felt letters, however powerfully illustrated, cannot be answered if they contain no postal address, and are, in effect, News From No-where. Bella dama alle pigiame rosse rilucentissime, Ischia, is hardly a proper direction for a respectable envelope.

I think you had better let Peter alone. He has inherited from you a reckless trick of playing on people's emotions, and has even developed a considerable technique in that direction. You do it from vanity and devilment; but he does it as a matter of business to gain his ends. As you dont like him it will cost you nothing to rule out this dangerous game in your dealings with him, and leave him to Lawrence and to himself.

I have come to the conclusion that he will be better able to take care of himself than either of you can take of him. Mild Mr Brown-rigg, once so confident that he could make a first rate British gentleman schoolboy of Peter (horrible doom!) has confessed that when he had Peter at home with him for the holidays he noticed, at these close quarters, that Peter's character was more egocentric than he had supposed. Your anecdote of the watches shews that Peter has a natural taste for making money breed. If only he will keep that taste within legal limits you need have no further anxi-ety about him: he may become the most successful (and worst) type of American; and he will never realize Mr B's ideal. It is too soon to be quite sure; for if you read the first act of Man and Superman you will be reminded that boys' consciences do not develop until their sex develops. A boy who will tell you bushels of lies without the slightest remorse at 12½ may be fiercely truthful at 15. Peter, now a scrapegrace, may be a Puritan presently. It is too soon to ~~admixix~~ attempt to class him.

On the whole I think that whether he develops a conscience or not, he had better be an American than a cosmopolitan vagabond. You are the very worst possible company for him; so keep him away from you. I have seen too much of the only sons of fascinating mothers to have any doubt about that. If when you are old you want to be maternally sentimental you can spoil his children.

It seems to me that if Lawrence's people would take him and see him through school and college (for a consideration, of course) that would be about the best send-off for him. In America young men are expected to have university degrees to qualify them for upper division jobs in business: in England an Oxford or Cambridge degree is the hallmark of a gentleman in society and of a duffer in business, where it is a positive drawback.

I think if a woman wants to be a mother she must keep a very regular house and play the game according to the ~~~~ general rule. If

she wants to be an artist and a vagabond, not to say a siren, she
should ponder the words of that great artist and poet William
Morris, who, though he kept his two houses most beautifully, said
to me "It is very difficult to decide who are the best people to
take charge of the children; but it is quite certain that the parents are the very worst". Some parents hold on to their children
because they regard them as their property and resent anyone else
touching them. Others hold on them from love of power over them,
and determination not to let them get free. But with all your
faults I dont think you feel that way about Peter; and Lawrence
would sink his feelings if he was convinced that it was for the
boy's good.

Anyhow,there the case stands: I can make no more of it.

You really have acquired a power of drawing; and I think your
line must be mainly portrait painting, because your invention does
not run into pictorial composition: what you imagine,you want to
act or write, not to compose into Raphael cartoons.

By the way, that play of Lawrence's was a remarkable effort.
I should say he was a born playwright if it were not that — just
as H.G.Wells says every man has one book in him: his own life —
every man has one play in him: his revenge on his wife. Probably
it is good for a woman to have her husband seize her by the scruff
of the neck; wash all the make-up off her face and the dye out of
her hair; and shove her nose against the mirror with a yell of
"There, you little ?????: that's what you really are. Look at
yourself". So he will have to write three or four more plays before
xsuxxxifxxxxxxxx I can decide whether it is his job.

That is all I have time for to-day.

                              G. Bernard Shaw

TELEGRAMS:
MALVERN HOTEL, MALVERN

TELEPHONE 338.

25th July 1935
Malvern Hotel,
Malvern.

My dear Molly

    I am down here rehearsing for the annual Festival. On my way hither I passed Stowe, but did not look up Peter, as I gathered from your letter that he was with you in Italy. But in any case I should probably not have bothered him ; for I have been particularly careful not to intrude on him and make him feel that he ought to write me duty letters and be grateful to me : in short, make him loathe my name to the end of his days.

    As they require a whole term's notice of the removal of a boy from Stowe, I shall have to pay for a term from the date of the notice ; so Peter can consider whether he had not better put in another term there since it will have to be paid for whether he does or not. However, if he does not feel that he getting any good out of the place, his going back would be the worst way of wasting the money.

    As all experiences have some sort of value, even that of having been at an English public school may come in handy. It is as well to know the artificial mentality which still characterizes the governing classes in England ; but it extremely undesirable to acquire that mentality ; and I entirely approve of Peter's escaping before he is pithed and turned out as a political and moral gentleman several centuries out of date. Georgia may be worse, and Harvard worse still; but they are American ; and I think Peter had better make up his mind to be an American planted on his native soil ; for anything is better than the vagabond artistic American of the nineteenth century, hanging round the picture galleries and talking Henry James or Frank Harris, accor ding to taste. He might begin by writing a novel in the manner of Waugh's Loom of Youth, entitled Adventures of a Stowe-away.

Tomorrow I enter my eightieth year; so you must set up a younger idol. I am not at all sure that old age is not the happiest phase of life. I dropped down dead last November ; but my heart for some reason (an inadequate one, I fear) began beating again after a while. I went to bed and slept for three days. I stayed in bed for four days more, and arose quite well. Next time my heart will be less officious and leave me an adored memory instead of an old dotard.

I still write plays and things. Do you still paint ? Brioni is all very well if you play polo and golf, and swim, or if you like playing water polo in a hot swimming bath before dinner and then sitting up all night gambling and drinking ; but you soon get tired of being confined in a private park, however lovely, and dash over to the mainland just to be in a street again among common crowds. I shall not revisit it. I now take my holidays on ships going as far round the world as possible, as I find that in this way alone can I work continuously and rest at the same time.

I notice that you say that Peter will leave England on the first ; so he was presumably still at Stowe when I passed. Lawrence, I take it, is still in Georgia making busts of the most remarkable men in America, who are ubiquitous in that country. I wonder how Peter will stand it.

Do not be sensitive about the money he costs. One of the first arts of life is to have no delicacy about money.

sempre a te G. Bernard Shaw

13th September 1935

TELEGRAMS:
MALVERN HOTEL, MALVERN.

TELEPHONE 338.

MALVERN HOTEL,
MALVERN.

My dear Molly

Your first letter, undated, and with no address but Trieste, said that you were stranded destitute, and that Peter had just sailed in the Conte Grandi, but of whither he sailed, Stowe or Georgia, not a syllable.

I infer from your second letter that you have managed to reach home, and that Peter has bidden farewell to Stowe, and is on the ocean.

From his dossier (which I am sending on to Laurence) I learn with a chuckle that he is peculiarly fitted for a position of authority as he has a strong regard for his own interests and none for those of other people. That is the British public school all over ; but I have never before seen it expressed with such cynical frankness.

American universities, with their campus activities and their appalling snobberies and conventionalities, have all the vices of English universities with a lower standard of learning ; and if Peter were a normal boy with a bent for Science or mathematics I should deplore the substitution of Atlanta for Cambridge ; but as it is, perhaps the greater variety of experience he gets, the better. One can only look on and wonder how he will turn out.

I spent some time in Brioni ; but as I am neither a golfer nor a polo fan it was a prison to me. I cannot stand being confined to a park, however picturesque ; and from time to time I had to make a dash over to the mainland to get into streets of all sorts of people and limitless roads. But for Gene Tunney and Richard Strauss I could not have en-

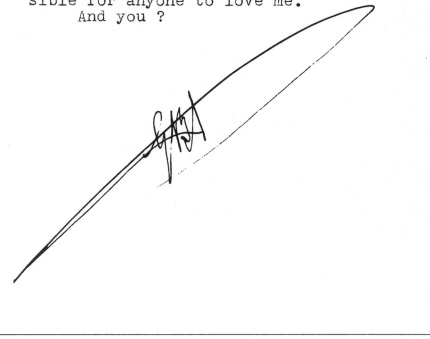

dured it. And the bora was the most horrible wind that ever blew, even in Italy. I should have been much happier at
Ragusa or Spalato.
       Do you continue to paint ? and do
your pictures sell ? Does Laurence make
busts of rich Georgians ; and how much
does he get for them ? I am so old and
gaga that I think my plays better than
ever, though not so thick ; but I am a
repulsive spectacle on the verge of
eighty ; and, as you perceive, I have
absolutely nothing to say. It is impossible for anyone to love me.
       And you ?

P.T. sailed for America, where he decided to spend a year in
his native Athens attending the University of Georgia before
going on to Harvard the following autumn.

AYOT ST LAWRENCE, WELWYN, HERTS. 24th November 1935.
STATION: WHEATHAMPSTEAD, G.N.R. 2¼ MILES.
TELEGRAMS: BERNARD SHAW, CODICOTE.   10 ADELPHI TERRACE. W.C.2.

My dear Molly

The change from stodgy Bucks to electric Georgia must have been
violent enough to upset a much less temperamental lad than Peter. But
if Lawrence keeps his pockets shut Peter will have to sell the Buick
and tighten his belt for the rest of the month, which will moderate his
ardor until he gets used to the climate.

Whether a man is fastidious about women or not depends a good
deal on the standard set him by his mother. To one whose mother is ugly
and hateful evry drab may seem an angel. An unusually attractive mother,
on the other hand, may prevent a man ever getting married, like Higgins
in Pygmalion. Peter is queerly placed between the two extremes. As to behavior you have been, during his most impressionable years, a savage ;
but you have been attractive in person, and quite idealizable to a child
too young to know the difference between disciplined social behavior and
barbarism.So let us hope that Peter will continue to be rather particular as to the quality of his seraglio.

I have no news about myself that is not public news. I am in my
eightieth year, and have to warn ladies with a Shaw fixation that they
must never get so fixed on another person as to be unable to do without him.
You must not decentralize yourself, fixation or no fixation. What
more can I say ?

An actress named Porboni, said to be one of Italy's young best,
whats to do a play of mine, Too True To Be Good, which is of all plays the
most impossible in a country at war. She would be sent to the Lipari islands. Therefore I have had to cut off all attempts to have my plays performed or licensed in Italy until the war is over.

Have you given up painting? Bridge is all very well financially if
you play well enough to win on balance in the year ; but my experience
is that people who take to bridge never do anything else.

My plays, though not so heavy as they used to be, have still bits
and scraps of fine stuff in them. But I am a dead man to the extent that
I find it extraordinarily difficult to write personal letters. So if I am
a bad and dull correspondent blame my years and not myself.

Does Lawrence find plenty of work in Georgia ?

come sempre

G.B.S.

168

AYOT ST LAWRENCE, WELWYN, HERTS. 21st Dec. 1934.
STATION: WHEATHAMPSTEAD, L.& N.E.R. 2¼ MILES.
TELEGRAMS: BERNARD SHAW, CODICOTE.
TELEPHONE: CODICOTE 18.

4, WHITEHALL COURT, LONDON, S.W.1.

My dear Molly

I havn't written a private letter for six months past.

We are now very old (over 80) and run away from everybody more exciting than very respectable couples over 60. We were just terrified to hear that you are in London. You mustnt come near us.

Still, I could just bear some news about you. I have heard that Lawrence has divorced you and is in New York. Of Peter, nothing. Of you, nothing. Next time you feel disposed to bring the story up to date in your incomparable narrative style, my ear, though now rather deaf, will be attentive and interested.

agedly

G. Bernard Shaw

Divorced by L.T., M.T. took a studio in Chelsea in order to spend a quiet winter in London painting. Suspended from Harvard for "sophistry," P.T. had enrolled at the Sorbonne in Paris.

From Bernard Shaw.

Fresco! Nonsense! you are not painting on wet plaster with water and lime to mix your colors and the plaster laid on day by day, are you? That, Molly, is fresco.

As you mention eggs I presume what you are working in is tempera. Have you read Cennini's treatise? In 1899 it was translated into English by Mrs. ~~Herring~~ Herringham. It set the painters using yolk of egg as well as white. Much more economical.

You must be having a happy time at last.

What does Peter mean by a transfer? What service is he in?

I dont think Italy a healthy place for young Americans. Dont let him work up a mother fixation. He had better stay where he is and get married.

G.B.S.

4, WHITEHALL COURT (130) LONDON, S.W.1. TELEGRAMS: SOCIALIST, PARL-LONDON. TELEPHONE: WHITEHALL 3160.

AYOT ST. LAWRENCE, WELWYN, HERTS. STATION: WHEATHAMPSTEAD, L & N.E.R., 2¼ MILES. TELEGRAMS AND PHONE: CODICOTE 218

28/6/29

The technique M.T. was using to decorate the walls of a Lombard castle was *fresco secco,* which requires eggs, flour, and sugar, the formulas for which M.T. learned from a Venetian in whose family the secret had been handed down from generation to generation. P.T. had transferred from the Sorbonne to Columbia University in order to be in New York.

170

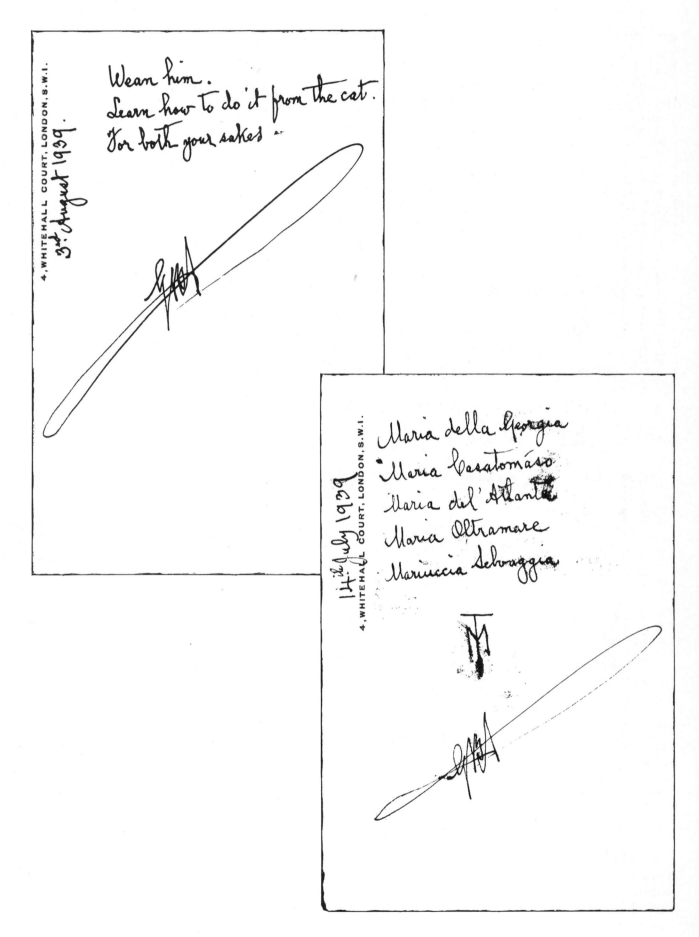

4, WHITEHALL COURT, LONDON, S.W.I.
3rd August 1939.

Wean him.
Learn how to do it from the cat.
For both your sakes —

4, WHITEHALL COURT, LONDON, S.W.I.
14th July 1939

Maria della Georgia
Maria Casatomáso
Maria del' Atlante
Maria Oltramare
Mariuccia Selvaggia

Hotel Esplanade. Frinton-on-Sea. Essex. England
20ᵗʰ Septʳ 1939.

Molli mia

Except that Apudo is your generous patron and host I am quite in the dark as to who your Riccardos and Guiseppes and Beppos and Giovannis may be. But it doesn't matter. I dismiss the poor lady with cancer from my mind as she is dead, and with her all the confusion of mind into which your narrative cast me.

In view of the mother fixation I advise you never to let Peter's wife, whoever she may be, enter your house, nor enter hers on any ground whatever. As to teaching her anything, of what use would your very personal methods, both in painting and housekeeping, be to her? Anyhow the relation of teacher and pupil is the very worst that could be set up between mother-in-law and daughter-in-law — always a difficult relation at best.

Until Peter has found his level, and is settled in it, it will be impossible to say what sort of wife would suit him. If this lady is an artist and is in love with him she had better provide a refuge for him by marrying some square toed man of business in comfortable circumstances, and taking on Peter as a Sunday husband. Cuckoos of that sort are quite an acquisition in a household if they are interesting, helpless, and innocent. Coleridge, for instance. Have you read the story of myself and May Morris?

I cannot understand Peter's move to Bordeaux. Why? He is an American citizen and a neutral, is he not? Italy is not in the war. What are you talking about?

I am here at the seaside until the 29ᵗ, when I return to Ayot. My wife has been very ill here. I am too much occupied to write, except professionally; but at 83 I can still read your letters

PS The proposed Memoires Galantes are horrifyingly out of the question. Only a very innocent boy could have conceived such a thing. You must really either get him married or persuade some experienced friend to educate him.

AYOT ST LAWRENCE, WELWYN, HERTS. 7th Nov. 1939   4, WHITEHALL COURT, LONDON, S.W.I.
STATION: WHEATHAMPSTEAD, L.& N.E.R. 2 MILES.
TELEGRAMS: BERNARD SHAW, CODICOTE.
TELEPHONE: CODICOTE 218.

Molly, Molly

I can make nothing of your letters unless you fill up the enclosed questionnaire for me. I should like to know also what alimony (if any) was decreed for you when your marriage was dissolved Is the divorce valid in the United States? Were you civilly married or in church?

You owe the lady an apology. Being a professional journalist I was paid for the article: at least an American newspaper proprietor sent me $ dollars the other day.

As you are not a politician, and other people are entitled to their opinions, You had better say in future that all you know about it is that people are always talking about me like that and always finding out a month later that I was quite right.

In the present case I am supporting the Duce's plea for an armistice and a conference. I was almost singlehanded when I declared for Italy in the Abyssinian affair. Italians who abuse me don't know what they are talking about.

Has Peter dropped that biography? He must. And you must cut the apron string.

174

4, WHITEHALL COURT (130) LONDON, S.W.1.

TELEGRAMS: SOCIALIST, PARL-LONDON.

TELEPHONE: WHITEHALL 3160.

AYOT ST LAWRENCE . WELWYN, HERTS.

STATION: WHEATHAMPSTEAD, L & N.E.R., 2¼ MILES.

TELEGRAMS AND PHONE: CODICOTE No 218

27-11-39.

From Bernard Shaw.

Your letter, posted on the 17th., reached me this morning on the 27th. It was opened by the French censorship, taking them ten days to read it, apparently.

I cannot send you printed documents of a political nature. They are contraband of war. I should have explained this.

It was very kind of Signor Picenardi to fill up my questionnaire and to understand that it was not an impertinence but a desperate attempt to find out what your letters were all about.

I have visited Venice three times. The third time it *bored* me !!! Get into a motor boat and go to Torcello and Chioggia. Dont attempt to look at the historical ceiling pictures in the Ducal Palace: there are so many that there had better be none at all. In the Scuola di S. Lucca there are just enough; but the lighting is bad.

You must learn the etiquette of the staircases if you have access on the go into noble society in Italy

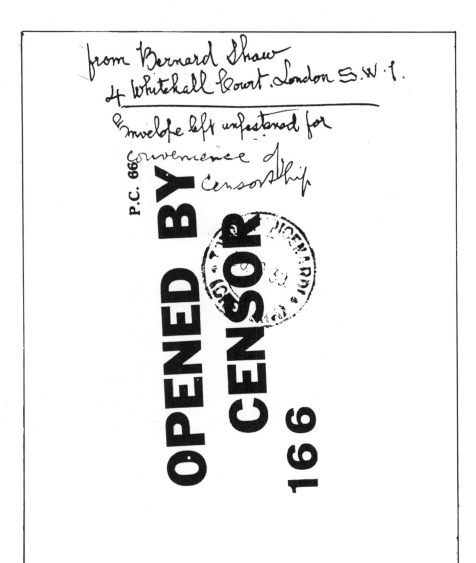

176

AYOT ST LAWRENCE, WELWYN, HERTS 22 May 1940.
STATION: WHEATHAMPSTEAD. L.& N.E.R. 2¼ MILES.
TELEGRAMS: BERNARD SHAW, CODICOTE.
4, WHITEHALL COURT, LONDON, S.W.1.

I have no news — am only glad that you are safe back in the Torre.

The Servudachi (?) lady has written me an appalling account of Troubetskoy's death. He fell into the fire and was burnt.

She seems to have affectionate recollections of you.

This is not a letter: only a sign of life.

Think of Peter being 21 !

EXAMINER 9094

BARNET
4 45 PM
8 NOV
1942
HERTS

Mrs Lawrence Tompkins
51 West 53rd St
New York City.

U. S. America

AYOT ST LAWRENCE, WELWYN, HERTS. 7/11/1942
STATION: WHEATHAMPSTEAD, L & N.E.R. 2¼ MILES.
TELEGRAMS: BERNARD SHAW, CODICOTE.
TELEPHONE: CODICOTE 218.

4, WHITEHALL COURT, LONDON, S.W.1.

My dear Molly

At last an address to which I can write.

That photograph in the cross word puzzle was taken in the St Joan year: 1924: eighteen years ago. It is a picture of a man of 68, still presentable. He is now in his 87th year, a ghastly old spectre who has outstayed his welcome, and would shock you and horrify Peter if he were inconsiderate enough to let you see him.

His wife, only 4 months younger, is an incurable invalid.

I can still read and even write quite a bit; so correspondence is possible, but not bodily vision or contact. The man you knew is dead.

And you, Molly: you must be 50. Do you keep your good looks?

And Lawrence? what of him? Is he in Atlanta? Has he married again?

What do you do with yourself? Paint? How did you escape from Italy?
I feared you were interned on the Lipari Islands.

Give me a scrap more news in your next — if you ever write it.

180

AYOT ST LAWRENCE, WELWYN, HERTS.
STATION: WHEATHAMPSTEAD, L.& N.E.R. 2¼ MILES.
TELEGRAMS: BERNARD SHAW, CODICOTE.
TELEPHONE: CODICOTE 18.

4th December 1944.

4, WHITEHALL COURT, LONDON, S.W.1.

My dear Molly

    I see you are settled at the same address as that of two
years ago, which I took to be a temporary one. Had I known, I should
have written.

    I am a vecchio, nearly eightyeight and a half. I am also a widower.
Charlotte died on the 12th September 1943. I was not in the least
grieved ; for she was only a year younger than I ; and it was
time for her to go; but I was very deeply moved. Her four years illness
thretened to have a dreadful end ; but a miracle intervened : she
suddenly became younger than I had ever seen her, and incredibly beati-
ful, and had thirty hours of ecstatic happiness before she ceased to
breathe. It was an unspeakable relief. The hundreds of letters I got
commiserating on my sorrow were all wrong. My health improved so much
that I realized that if she had lived another year she would have killed
us all, though we were not conscious of the strain while we were under
it. I have had some offers of marriage since, as I am rather a
catch now, having only a few years at most to live (quite probably a
few days) and my widow would be well provided for, though the terrific
war taxation and the death duties on Charlotte's property have left me
far poorer than people think.

    But I have had enough of marriage, and am quite happy alone, as I
inherit from my mother a great capacity for solitude in my own company.

    Tell Pete that to hoard money, or waste it, or neglect to invest
it in socially useful enterprises, or at least lend it to the State,
is a crime of which no Socialist, and certainly no Shavian, should be
guilty.

    You do not tell me what Pete has been doing or where he has been
all this time. Nor do you say a word about Lawrence's work. He should
be recognized by this time as a very cosiderable scupltor. By the way, I
hope you two have had the good sense to marry again : that silly divorce
will make no end of trouble later on unless it is got rid of.
Do you keep your good looks still ? I can still write a bit, with

many blots and blunders (the book has ~~however~~ at least thirty howlers in it) ; and I can produce a stage effect of being sound in wind and limb, though a trifle deafish ; but really I am a not very majestic ruin.

"All your Italian friends must be starving now that we have "liberated" them. Albert and Madelon, now no longer man and wife, are well out of it. Cecil Lewis has married again, this time apparently quite comfortably. He has managed to hold on to his villa on the Maggiore, but is too busy in the Air Force to go back there yet.

What is Pete's branch of military service. A spell of discipline in corporative service is probably good for him after his anarchical bringing-up. Or has he been a war correspondent all the time? How old is he now?

Let me have a line occasionally. We can write more freely now that Charlotte can never read our letters. ~~never~~ As I have more letters in a week than I can deal with in a month dont mind if my answers are belated. Take care they dont get out of your hands. Journalists regard letters by me as their natural prey.

Goodnight. I can now go to bed as late as I please.

G. Bernard Shaw

never I could bring myself to write a line that could hurt her; but now I can write anything.

11/9/1945
**AYOT ST LAWRENCE
Nr WELWYN
HERTS**

Letter will follow when I have time to write it.

I did answer Peter; but I could not send him the books because they are all (including most of my own) out of print through the paper shortage. Besides, damn him! I have no time for office boy's jobs — buying books and making up parcels. And if he expects replies from me by return of post he will be bitterly disappointed. My most pressing correspondents are lucky if they hear within two years. Even you, dear Molly!

In Berlin with an advance guard of the OSS, and dealing with the Russians, P.T. had written Shaw for some hard-to-find books.

Spoilt by the blob of red ink; but I send it because it shews my full front face just as it now is. The other gives my profile. Both, alas! are only too like me.

11/9/45

1945

G. B. S.

Gabriel Pascal
Hungarian Film Artist

Georges Auric
French composer.

at Ayot Saint Lawrence, discussing the filming of Caesar and Cleopatra

AYOT ST LAWRENCE, WELWYN, HERTS.
STATION:WHEATHAMPSTEAD,L.&N.E.R.2¼ MILES.
TELEGRAMS: BERNARD SHAW, CODICOTE.
TELEPHONE: CODICOTE 18.

30th October 1945

4,WHITEHALL COURT, LONDON, S.W.I.

My dear Molly
        I have just received your letter, with its proposal to come across the ocean to live with me. The same idea has occurred to other women.Put it out of your very inconsiderate head at once and forever, as they have had to. No woman shall ever live with me again in that sense.
        I am a Great Man, living in dignified retirement in a village in a house which I have given to the National Trust to keep as a memorial of my life here with Charlotte and my death in a solitude which let nobody dare to profane. It is kept for me by a treasure of a stern Scottish housekeeper who is quite indispensable to me. If you arrived and proposed to settle in for a single night she would leave me instantly ; and our devoted Irish Catholic housemaid would follow her and make the house un-inhabitable. The scandal in the village, the degradation to Literature, the insult to Charlotte's memoery memory would be such that I should be justified in shooting you if there no other way of preventing you from crashing my gates.
        If you nevertheless try, it will not be necessary to shoot you ; but the Irish maid will say"Not at home"; and you will never see me or hear from me again.
        Why have you not known all this without my having to tell you? You are no longer a young savage: you are a mature woman. If you ever think of old men of ninety, you must realize that they do not wish to be made ridiculous, much less disgraced before all the world. Anyhow, dear Molly. you know now ; so enough of the ssubject.
        You have left me no time to say more. You never tell me anything about Lawrence's career as a sculptor, as to which I am interested and curious. And though Peter turns up in your letters at moments I cannot make out where he is nor what he is nor anything definite. Still it is cheering to know that you are painting away busily, as this inplies that you may be making a success of it artistically if not commercially. There are worse places to live in than a barge. Let me know sometimes how you are getting on ; but no more atomic bombs, please.

                                G.B.S.

From
Bernard Shaw

Phone & Wire:
CODICOTE 218.

8ᵗʰ Dec. 1946

**AYOT SAINT LAWRENCE,
WELWYN,
HERTS,**

My dear Molly

Your letters knock me endways. I am too old for such shocks.

You a shop assistant! And in Brentanos whom I helped to bankrupt years ago. Is there anyone of that name still in the business? One of the old stock is very angry with me just now. So be careful.

Of course you will come to the top like a cork. Brains like yours are scarce in business. And the employment will be good for you.

Tell me definitely does Lawrence go on with his sculpture. If he doesn't he will go mad.

I did not know that you were one of F-R's numerous infatuations.

What became of the Italian feudal aristocrat whose castle you were frescoing?

G. B. S.

F-R is, of course, Forbes-Robertson; the aristocrat Marchese Guido Sommi-Picinardi, who died in 1950.

From
Bernard Shaw

Phone & Wire:
CODICOTE 218. 3/7/1948   AYOT SAINT LAWRENCE,

WELWYN,

HERTS.

My dear Molly

You have sent me a letter written on tran-
parent tissue paper on both sides, the back
obliterating the front. Do you expect me to
decipher it ?

All I can make out is that you are in Rome
with Peter's family ; that Peter has been called away to Athens ; that you are companion to
an old lady who pays you nothing except the
cost of a Cunard passage on which you saved
something by coming on a freighter ; and that ▮▮
Lawrence cannot do without you and will not▮▮▮▮▮
▮▮▮▮▮▮▮▮▮remarry you.

Do you realize that I am 92, and that I ▮▮
can no longer be of any use or interest to you
or to anyone else¡ If not, the enclosed card
will convince you. Drop me ; and make young
friends.

G.B.S.

From
Bernard Shaw

Phone & Wire:
CODICOTE 218.   8/2/1949

AYOT SAINT LAWRENCE
WELWYN, HERTS.

My dear Molly

My life now passes in a routine that never changes and has no events (outside my professional work) that have any interest for anyone but myself. In short, no news.

You must cast me off like a laddered stocking, and get a younger correspondent.

Dont think, however, that I am forgetting you. I have two things to urge.

First, you must make Lawrence remarry you. If he cannot do without a wife and a model he should pay the market price for them. If he died where would you be? Strike for a wedding ring and a settlement.

Second, tell Peter that Montessori is all right while the children are under six, but no use afterwards. So the Italian nuns say; and it is exactly what one would expect. So he must look ahead and not imagine that the education problem is disposed of.

Are the infants to grow up Italians or Americans? Small things pick up languages and throw them off like hips and haws, but not grown-ups.

There is money in directing and designing rug-making, but not in putting in the stitches. Employ the stitchers and weavers; buy the wools and sell the rugs; but, except for fun, keep yourself by your head, not by your hands. No room for more.

G.B.S.

In Rome for the Columbia Broadcasting System P.T. was sending his three-year-old son and four-year-old daughter to a Montessori day school.

From Bernard Shaw.

4, WHITEHALL COURT (130) LONDON, S.W.I.
TELEGRAMS: SOCIALIST, PARL-LONDON.
PHONE: WHITEHALL 3160.

Ayot Saint Lawrence
Welwyn, Herts.

26th March 1949

My dear Molly,

What you say on the remarriage question would be all right if you were living apart and the marriage were an abandoned failure. But it is nothing of the sort. You are in daily intercourse as much as if you were married; and there is no excuse whatever for either of you refusing or even hesitating to regularize the situation for the sake of Peter and his children as well as for your own sake in the event of Lawrence's death.

And Lawrence will die of the unsettlement and worry of his present position, though he is not conscious that it is killing him.

So let me have no more nonsense about it; but do as I tell you, both of you.

You cannot live by tapestry except as an employer training his staff of executant employees to do the hand work your designs.

In great haste: I can hardly snatch a moment for private letters.

Mrs Lawrence Tompkins,
51 West 53rd Street
New York City 19
U.S.America.

190

The Old Man at his gate
As he was in fortyeight
And still is at ninety three
Awaiting news of thee
                    Molly Bawn

18765. Ayot Saint Lawrence
            3 January 1949

POSTSCRIPT

There were two more letters after this, but when M.T. moved to Atlanta, Georgia, where L.T. chose to settle not far from the house in which he was born, they were lost.

No matter. Though they may turn up someday with one or more of the earlier ones and fill the gaps in continuity, they are unlikely to affect the heart of what is here concluded.

Shaw died in November 1950.

Whether it was wisdom or rashness that prompted two young Americans to travel to England in the twenties to seek an ancient prophet and propagate his gospel is academic now; but as Shaw's ashes were being scattered on the lawn of Ayot St. Lawrence a leading twentieth-century statesman was to comment that though his plays are laughed at and enjoyed all over the world few people pay heed to the "deep lesson which his writing contains."